Nasty Norfolk: Scary Stories and Ghastly Ghosts

written and illustrated by
TREVOR HEATON

cover illustration Tony Hall

BOSWORTH
BOOKS

www.bosworthbooks.co.uk

Published by Bosworth Books,

Rose End, High Street, Whissonsett, Dereham, Norfolk NR20 5AP

First published in the UK by Bosworth Books 2007

www.bosworthbooks.co.uk

Text, design and illustrations copyright Trevor Heaton, 2007

Cover illustration copyright Tony Hall, 2007

Educational consultants: Julie Dicks BA (Hons), PGCE

and Velma Heaton BA (Hons), PGCE

ISBN 0-9551153-3-7 (978-0-9551153-3-2)

Printed and bound by Biddles Ltd, 24 Rollesby Road, Hardwick Industrial Estate,

King's Lynn, Norfolk PE30 4LS

NO HISTORY TEACHERS, GHOSTS, OR LARGE BLACK SCARY DOGS WERE INJURED

DURING THE MAKING OF THIS BOOK

Contents

Introduction

Think we've covered all the smelly, rotten, nasty bits of the county's past in **NASTY NORWICH** and **NASTY NORFOLK**?

Then think again, because we've delved once more into the dim and distant past to bring you some more! Only this time round we've gone for the scary as well as the pongy.

The foulest folklore, the rottenest rascals, the spookiest spirits and the ghastliest ghosts - we've got them lined up for you in the final instalment of our 'Chronicles of Nastier'.

And they are all true stories. Well, they might be. They are certainly truly scary. Some of them are modern, some are hundreds of years old.

And we've been dipping back into the past too for more of those nasty, quirky little stories that you wished your teachers would tell you....

Now it's time to read on – if you dare!

Spooky Schools

It's not just the terrible teachers* that make school a scary place. Oh no. For our first visit to the frightening side of Nasty Norfolk let's hear about two schools where there were a lot more things to worry about than double-PE on a wet Monday in November.

Oh yes there were...

*(*they're not all bad. No, really)*

Knock three times...
Our first tale comes from the early part of the last century, around the 1920s and 1930s. There used to be a school in Norwich called the Girls' Model School, which was near St Andrew's Church.

One of its former pupils told in 1971 about a strange and spooky thing which happened when she was there - so strange that all the class had been sworn to secrecy and it had taken her all this time before she felt she could talk about it.

One day the pupils were sitting in the classroom when there came three knocks at the door.

The teacher asked one of the pupils to open the door. There was no-one there. The teacher, annoyed, decided it was someone messing about and went back to the lesson.

Then someone knocked on the door again: tap, tap, tap.

The teacher, really annoyed this time, ordered the door opened again.

And once again, there was no-one there.

'Right,' thought the teacher. 'I'll really catch them next time and when I do, I'll *[the rest of this sentence has been censored for the sake of sensitive children's ears]*.'

So the teacher got three girls to stand by the door - one inside the large cupboard by the door (just in case there was someone messing about with that), one with her hand on the handle ready to open it, and the third ready to dash out in the corridor to catch the trickster.

After a few moments, the sound came again: *tap, tap, tap.*

Instantly, the door was flung open and a girl ran out in the corridor to catch the culprit. There was nowhere to hide.

But there was nobody in the corridor. There was nobody running down the stairs.

There was nobody there at all.

Frightened, the teacher told the class to keep quiet about the incident.

Was it the wind rattling the handle? Or a practical joke? No-one ever found out, and no-one ever owned up.

The Curse of the Mummy

The Great Yarmouth historian Clifford Temple used to tell a scary little story about a school in the town which had the mummy of an Egyptian princess in a casket in the science room.

Gradually, teachers and staff began to notice a bit of a pong – which they blamed it on the long-dead Egyptian (well, you would, wouldn't you?).

The decision was made to bury the casket's contents in the nearby churchyard.

So a grave was quickly dug and Princess Ancient was taken out of the casket and put inside the hole and covered up.

'Phew,' the teachers thought. 'That's the end of that.'

But after a day or two people kept hearing a knocking sound.

They searched everywhere but couldn't find where it was coming from. It wasn't outside or from the house next door.

Then someone went into the science room and realised there was still a smell coming from the casket. It was opened up and staff discovered...

...the Princess' leg, which had been left behind. The leg was quickly taken outside and buried with the rest of the long-dead Egyptian.

And the knocking sound? It stopped and never came back.

The spooky stories aren't just about the schools themselves. In the mid-1950s - still in Yarmouth - it was reported that 'some time ago' there had been something very strange happening in the old education offices on the South Quay. A member of staff had seen the figure of an elderly man coming down the stairs... but without making a single sound.

The man then vanished into thin air. When the staff started talking about what had happened one of the cleaners came forward to say she had seen the same thing happen. After investigations it was realised that the figure was very much like a man called Daniel Tomkins who used to run a college on the site...

The Brown Lady of Raynham

For our next story let's meet one of Norfolk's most famous ghosts. It's a story going back almost 300 years... and even scared a future king.

It all began, so the story goes, in the early 18th century when Dorothy Walpole - sister of the first prime minister Sir Robert Walpole - was forced to marry a much older man, the Marquis of Townshend. Her husband turned out to be a cruel and horrible man and eventually came up with a terrible way to get rid of her - by building a wall ... with her stuck, still alive, behind it.

He then staged a pretend funeral to make everyone believe she had died of natural causes.

But the dead Dorothy wasn't going to go quietly. Her spirit began to flit around the oak staircase at Raynham Hall.

The ghost of Dorothy was a terrible sight, dressed in velvet with [gulp!] empty eye sockets.

When the Prince Regent - the future George IV - came to stay at the hall he was said to have had a spooky encounter with the Brown Lady.

9

He was so scared he left early the next morning, saying: 'I will not pass another hour in this accursed house, for I have seen that what I hope to God I may never see again.'

But another version of the story has him just asking for another room - so perhaps he wasn't *that* scared.

The next celebrity ghost-spotter was the Victorian writer Captain Marryat, who reportedly fired a pistol at the Brown Lady.

The shot passed straight through the ghost and hit the door instead.

The writer Walter Rye, reporting in 1896, described the apparition as 'a little lady all dressed in brown, with dishevelled hair and a face of ashy paleness'.

There were more sightings in the 20th century. Around 1927 members of the Swaffham Amateur Players stayed overnight at the hall after giving an entertainment there. Three of them stayed in a room reputed to be haunted.

In the morning they were shocked to see that the sofa had the impression of a human figure in it. You see, none of them had slept on it...

Then in 1936 a photographer took a famous picture of the

'Well, it certainly made an impression on him...'

stairs which appeared to show a mysterious hooded figure on it. Was this the Brown Lady?

So far, so spooky. But historians say the idea of Dorothy Walpole being walled up is a silly one and that what evidence there is points to her having been happily married.

Her death (aged 40 in 1726) was blamed on smallpox, a common cause of death at the time, and was not due to anything sinister.

But the mystery of the Brown Lady of Raynham looks like it will be around for some while yet...

The Brown Lady is the most famous ghost of Raynham Hall, but she might not have been alone.

Lilias Rider Haggard, daughter of the Victorian adventure story writer Sir Henry Rider Haggard, lived at Ditchingham Hall, near Diss. She was a distant relation of the Townshends and she inherited a little oak figure of a housemaid with broom in hand.

The story was that the housemaid was at Raynham Hall where she was treated cruelly by the mother of the house - so she drowned herself.

From that day she could be heard along the corridors of Raynham Hall, sweeping. Backwards and forwards, backwards and forwards....

Haunted Halls

Raynham Hall isn't the only posh spooky place. Far from it. For almost everywhere in Norfolk where there's an old hall, there's a ghost story to go with it.

Here's a few of them...

Another scary lady

We've met the Brown Lady. Now let's say hello to the Grey one.

Dame Armine Le Strange was a member of the famous Le Strange family of Old Hunstanton who we first met in 'NASTY NORFOLK'. She lived in the 18th century and the biggest worry of her life was her son Nicholas, who was a terrible gambler.

As she lay dying she made Nicholas promise that he would never, *ever* sell her pride and joy - a beautiful Persian carpet.

Nicholas, to make absolutely sure he didn't break his promise, shut the precious carpet in a chest - and nailed it down. And to be fair to Nicholas, he kept his word.

It was still there when Nicholas himself died in 1788.

'Of course I won't sell this - I'll bet you'

The chest lay, dusty and forgotten until 1868 when Emmeline Austin, the new wife of the latest owner of the hall, Bernard Le Strange, found it.

She thought she would do all the poor people living in the cottages on the estate a favour by chopping up this old carpet and giving them a piece.

But as she came back to the hall she was startled to look up and see a figure in grey, looking down on her - and scowling.

Since then, the Grey Lady has put in more appearances, being described as 'like a restless fury, striking terror into the hearts of those who encountered her'. A housekeeper saw her around 1910 - and then there were stories of rattling chains being heard in the 1930s.

Sadly, the hall itself was hit badly by a series of fires. And so the Grey Lady had nowhere to haunt....

The strange encounter of Dr Jessopp...

Dr Augustus Jessopp was an important figure in Norfolk society in Victorian times - a clergyman, schoolmaster and writer. So when he said he'd seen something *very* strange at Mannington Hall, near Aylsham, people sat up and took notice - and made it one of the county's most talked-about tales.

Dr Jessopp told his audience in 1884 how, when he was reading alone in the library at the hall, he suddenly became aware of a tall priest-like figure beside him.

A large white hand from the figure came close to his elbow.

Surely the good vicar had seen a ghost?

Lots of people thought so, although 70 years later there was a series of letters in the Eastern Daily Press which claimed that Dr Jessopp must have dozed off and woken up to see the figure of Carlo, a servant. But other writers said this couldn't have happened.

The truth, like so many of our stories, will never be known.

...and the Rev R W Vaughan

It happened at Costessey Hall, a once-grand stately home near Norwich which has now been demolished. The Rev RW Vaughan was sitting in the library when he met an ancient-looking figure in a dark velvet coat two nights running.

The second time, the young vicar plucked up the courage to ask the ghost if he needed any help.

The spirit told him he was a Roman Catholic priest who had been hearing a confession but had been forced to hide it in a book when some Protestant priest-hunters turned up.

Later the priest had left England and died without ever having the chance to find the confession and destroy it. He gave the startled young cleric the instructions about when he could find - and destroy - the document.

So the Rev Vaughan did just that - and the ghost was at peace at last.

That's not the only story about the hall, once home to the Jerningham family and a place which used to be so grand that the future Edward VII once came to stay.

Only the belfry tower remains as the last tiny fragment of the hall - but even that fragment has a tale to tell. The ghost of a lady dressed in green is supposed to haunt there.

The two ghost children
Here's a couple of stories about two junior spooks.

The first story comes from 1897, when it was reported that the ruined Harling Old Hall had a sinister secret - the ghost of a child.

' "Water" terrible fate this is...'

The child was the daughter of the owner of the house and one of his servant girls. She died when she fell - or was it pushed? - into the moat. She obviously reckoned she was pushed, because her spirit came back to haunt the hall.

But the ghost of Ashwellthorpe Hall, as reported in 1969, seems altogether happier.

It's a cheeky little girl dressed in a red cloak who hides keys and switches lights on.

Nothing too spooky there then. But that's not the case with our next haunting...

Ghostly Gawdy
Our next story takes us to 1665, when Gawdy Brampton of Blo' Norton Hall lived happily with his much younger second wife. But then Brampton made the mistake of getting involved with gambling, eventually losing his entire estate to his best friend. Overcome with guilt, he hanged himself.

And his spirit is said to flit around his old bedroom and climb the stairs, one creepy step after another...

Rotten rooms

Some halls have certain rooms that people will swear are haunted - but sooner or later someone is brave (or stupid!) enough to spend a night there.

Like Edward Harbord, who agreed to spend a night in the haunted bed-chamber at the (now demolished) Thursford Hall, which dated back to Elizabethan times. He made sure he had plenty of candles - so no-one could sneak in and play tricks - and, just to make sure, he locked the door.

He also kept two loaded pistols to hand.

All was quiet until, just before midnight, he heard footsteps on the stair outside - and suddenly the locked door flew open.

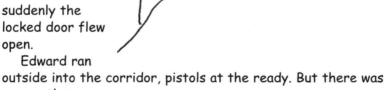

Edward ran outside into the corridor, pistols at the ready. But there was no-one there...

Sometimes the haunted room is sealed up (as is said to have been the case at Tharston Hall, near Long Stratton).

Terrible tales were told of the sealed-up room at Hasset Hall, which used to stand near Barrack Road in Norwich but was knocked down sometime in the 18th century.

Daniel Gurney wrote in 1820 that an old person had told him: 'My brother was, when young, in the Hall and saw an apparition of a dead body roll across the room.

'There is a closet in the old mansion that had never been opened and no-one knew what was there and the doors of the two rooms were plastered up, in attempting to open which two people had been struck blind.'

And this isn't all the Hasset Hall spooks - we'll meet another in the next chapter.

All White on the night

We've met Brown, Grey and Green Ladies. Now let's say hello to a White one.

The mysteriously-named White Woman Lane in Norwich is said - in one story anyway - to have got its strange name from the ghost of a bride from Catton Hall, who was murdered on her wedding night.

Her spirit used to flit along the lane.... until modern houses started being built there, and which seem to have driven her away.

Another white ghost (although a man this time) was said to have haunted the site of the old Elizabethan hall which used to stand at Letton, near Dereham.

An old ash tree marked the start of a nightly walk of the figure in white, who walked up and down the road by the hall until vanishing as soon as dawn came.

It's a story which goes back to at least the 1850s.

The final ghost...by a whisker

Let's finish this chapter with the story of one of Norfolk's most unusual ghosts - a cat.

'Aaaaah,' I can hear you say, 'how sweet!'

But the story behind the phantom puss of Lynford Hall, near Mundford, isn't a very cuddly one.

The story goes like this. The daughter of a former owner of the house used to keep Persian cats secretly. Her father, you see, detested cats and had forbidden her to keep them.

So when he found out, he was so furious that took out his gun and shot them.

Since then, the phantom cat has turned up several times, and was spotted in the 1920s.

Our next helping of spooks also features animals. Er, but not exactly cuddly ones....

Gulp!

Cursed coaches

There's no doubt what the most popular sort of ghost is in Norfolk. For centuries spectral coach and horses have been rattling up and down lonely lanes, round country estates and even in and out of ponds.

They always seem to know where they're going, which is clever because the horses usually don't have any heads. And it's no good asking the coachman or the passengers to steer because - you've guessed it - they don't have heads either!

Let's meet some, shall we?

Scary Sir Thomas
Everyone knows the story of Henry VIII's unlucky queen Anne Boleyn. Henry divorced his first wife to marry the pretty young Anne - but within a couple of years Henry had got tired of her, accused her of all sorts of nasty crimes... and had her head chopped off.

Anne may have been born at Blickling Hall, near Aylsham, (or, rather, an earlier hall

'Henry did say I was a pain in the neck...'

which stood on the same site) which explains why her ghost is said to come up the driveway on the anniversary of her execution (May 19 1536) in a coach and horses, with the tragic queen carrying her severed head under her arm.

But Anne's ghost isn't the only boneless Boleyn. Her father, Sir Thomas, is supposed to have been cursed to ride on the same night, head tucked under his arm and spouting flames of fire.

His coach and horses has to travel over a certain number of bridges (some say 12, some say 40, as far afield as Wroxham and Coltishall) before the cock crows the dawn. That's the only way, you see, Sir T gets to have a year off his haunting duties.

And just to hurry him along a bit there's a few screaming demons chasing him too!

There's a story that a farmworker was once hurrying home on the fateful anniversary and was just crossing a bridge when he heard the unmistakeable sound of the ghost coach come up fast behind him.

He heard Sir Thomas shouting out for him to open the gate, but the man knew that if he turned his head to look at the terrible transport, then he would be pulled on board... as a passenger.

Sir Thomas is supposed to have been cursed to ride round for 1,000 years. So if you've missed out on the spooky spectacle, don't worry... you've always got another, oh, 520-odd years or so to spot him!

And Sir T and Lady A aren't the only Blickling residents to have a habit of stirring. The story goes that the Blickling Mausoleum was built to house coffins because every time the family vault in the church was opened for a new burial, the coffins would have mysteriously moved, all by themselves....

The perilous poachers
That farmworker who refused to look at Sir Thomas' coach was no fool. It's always been a very bad idea to gaze on the galloping ghosts.

Just ask George Mace. Oh, hang on a minute, you can't - he's dead.

It happened like this. George was the leader of a gang of poachers in the 19th century who arranged to meet near Breckles Hall, not far from Watton. Everyone had arrived at the agreed place - except Mace.

They looked for him, but couldn't find him anywhere.

Then suddenly they heard the sound of wheels and a ghostly coach arriving. The terrified poachers could hear the sounds of a door being opened and closed suddenly and then - nothing.

The gang ran away, frightened. They crept back the next morning and found George Mace by the front door of the ancient hall.

Dead.

And the story goes that the opening and closing of the door was the sound of his soul being taken away to Hell...

Meanwhile, across the county at Spixworth a hearse (funeral coach) and four black horses - but no driver - haunt the main road through the village. It's certain death if it's spotted. A farmer in Victorian times made the mistake of doing that - and was dead within a week.

More misfortune follows if you spot the phantom coach on the old Norwich road at Great Melton.

It contains four headless bridesmaids with a headless coachman driving the horses.

They are said to haunt the area because they were murdered there by a highwayman.

Another version of the story has it that the coach slipped off the road one dark night and fell into a bottomless pool.

Every now and then, at midnight, the coach rises silently from the water - dripping wet - and travels round the field before sinking into the pool again. Glug, glug, glug...

And talking about unlucky weddings, there's similar stories told about a pond called Bride's Pit in Swaffham, and the Lily Pit, by Beccles Road at Gorleston supposed, as far back as 1874, to be 'haunted by evil spirits'...

One person who saw a phantom coach and lived to tell the tale was Sam Baldwin.

He was walking along the road from Pulham Market to Rushall around 1817 when he heard a coach and horses coming up fast behind him.

He quickly stepped out of the way - and was shocked to see it was being driven by a headless coachman, cracking a fiery whip.

Then there's the story of the woman from Cranworth who told a Mrs Gurdon in the late 19th century how she, too, had seen a phantom coach.

It happened when she was a teenager:

'I was in bed when I heard a kind of heavy rumbling a-coming down the road.

'I went to the window and there I saw it plainly - a coach with bright lamps, an' the windows lit up as bright as day, and all ablaze with light. I could see right plain, an' it moved fast, but there were no horses in it...'

The coach went as far as the turning for Woodrising - and vanished.

More ghostly coach stops!

If it is just the one ghostly coach making all these calls then, boy, has it got a busy timetable!

It's been reported at Hoveton sometime in the 1820s and 1830s (when it was so bright as it rushed by a startled cart-owner that he could see every nail in his wagon - at midnight), West Dereham (New Year's Eve), Lovell's Hall in Terrington St Clement, our old friends Lynford Hall and Hasset Hall, while over at Caistor Castle the headless coach'n'horses turns up once every year and rushes round the courtyard.

Phew!

...And a foul footnote

A headless horseman was seen in the lanes around Fakenham in the Victorian era (wondering where his coach had disappeared to, probably).

But over at Trowse it was a phantom white horse (and no rider) which was seen in 1912. The sighting was linked to the tale of a young mother who had ventured out on the ice... only for it to suddenly crack and pitch her into the freezing river....

The last word belongs to Letton. Or should that be 'the last bray'.

Because in Victorian time it was believed the village was haunted by... a headless donkey.

And just in case you think that doesn't sound too bad, just listen to what Emily Cranworth had to say in 1900.

'I heard of the donkey in another house in the village, where the farmer's wife tells with shuddering horror how she was out late at night, some years back, when suddenly she felt a cold shiver run down her back, and she heard steps coming behind her so closely that it seemed as though they must tread upon her heels.

'Has somebody – anybody – seen my body?'

'She was much frightened, and she tried to peer back over her shoulder, but she saw in this half glance a shape close behind her, like a donkey standing on its hind legs, prancing and towering over her.

'She hurried on for her life, and the footsteps followed closely after her all the way until she reached home...'

Phew! That's quite enough nasty creatures for now, don't you think? Sorry, what was that - you'd like some more? How about the most famous one of them all...

Let's get ready to meet... BLACK SHUCK!

Tales of the Devil Dog

Scary Shuck

Every now and again it wasn't the sound of ghostly hooves and the rattle of coach wheels which made late-night walkers start running in terror.

It was the pad-pad-pad of giant paws - the feet of East Anglia's devil dog - Black Shuck!

Black Shuck is perhaps the most famous Norfolk legend of them all.

In fact it's so famous that it might have helped inspire the creator of Sherlock Holmes, Sir Arthur Conan Doyle, to come up with his idea of a sinister giant dog in The Hound of the Baskervilles (one of the most famous detective stories ever written).

We should say at this stage that Suffolk also has a claim to the phantom pooch, with visits to Bungay and Blythburgh in 1577 among others.

Black Shuck is the devil dog's most popular name, but it's been called lots of things over the years: Old Scarfe, Old Shuck, Shuck Dog, Skeff or just plain Shuck...

The name may be different, but the appearance of the dog spells one thing: trouble!

Black Shuck = Bad Luck

It's always been very bad news to see old Black Shuck - and not just because he's scary. It's even more sinister than that.

Broads writer Ernest Suffling wrote in the early 1890s how there was a tradition that if you saw Shuck you would die within 12 months.

But if you managed to keep it a secret for the whole year and not tell a soul, then you would live.

Pooch on patrol
Black Shuck's favourite pastime has traditionally been running from Cromer to Overstrand and back again every night with his head over his shoulder.

But he pops up in lots of places: Wells, Sheringham, Coltishall bridge, Hempnall, Marshland, Little Snoring and Geldeston to name but a few.

A man named Finch had a nasty surprise just under 200 years ago at Neatishead. He was walking along a lane when he saw a dog belonging to another villager which had snapped at him several times.

When the dog came bounding along the lane towards him, Finch thoughtto himself: 'Aha! This is where I get my revenge!'

So he lined up a great big kick, swung his foot and... was shocked to find it 'went through him like a sheet of paper'.

Of course, it wasn't the village dog - it was Shuck!

At Garvestone in the 19th century the spectre was known as Skeff, and one old gamekeeper once described him. 'His eyes are as big as saucers and blaze wi' fire.

'He is a fair big as a small pony, and his coat is a shaggy coat across, like an old sheep.

'He has a lane, and a place out of which he come, and he vanish when he's gone far enough.'

Around 1850 a Norfolk coroner was returning home in Marshland and was travelling along a road bordered on each side with ditches.

He noticed his horse was shaking with what seemed like fear, so he ordered his groom to stop.

Just then, 'a waft of cold dank air struck both men as in the light of the lamps a large black dog of supernatural size passed over the road from ditch to ditch in front of the trembling little mare.'

The Stiffkey scare

There's been lots of folklore handed down about Black Shuck. But, incredibly, in 1927 author Christopher Marlowe claimed he had actually been *chased* by the dog while walking on the marshes at Stiffkey one evening.

As he strolled along he became aware of an 'indefinable shadow' nearby. And then...

'The eerie silence was rent by the most appalling howl to which I have ever listened - it froze the blood in my veins and caused my hair to stand on end.'

Marlowe ran for his life to the cottage where he was staying.

As he reached it he banged desperately on the door to be let in, and only dared to look around as the door bolt was being slid back to let him in.

'I glanced round to see a pair of ferocious eyes fixed upon me and to feel on my neck a scorching... I fell fainting into the arms of my host.'

The devil dog's kennel?

At Southtown Road in Great Yarmouth the devil dog was called Old Scarfe. It pulled a chain and rushed up and down the road.

If a straw were laid across its path it would stop and howl 'like no other creature on Earth'...

But the story goes that a priest managed to force it to stay in a vault under the Duke's Head Inn on the quayside. And there it is doomed to remain 'until the river ceases to run under Yarmouth bridge'.

So have we heard the last of Black Shuck?

I wonder...

Shuck's friends

In any case, Black Shuck has a couple of animal pals to help him out.

If you go along the road between Kelling and Salthouse, so the story goes, you might just see a blue sow (female pig), while over in the Brecks area near Thetford Warren you need to keep your eyes peeled for the dreaded... White Rabbit!

Yes, the scary bunny has large flaming eyes and can hop after you very, very fast.

And just in case any mums and dads out there think this sounds a big too much like the killer rabbit from Monty Python and the Holy Grail, we should point out this story dates back to at least 1925. Yes, really!

'Orrible Oliver

Long memories...
Archaeologist Robin Brown told in 1979 how, some years earlier, he had been chatting to a villager from Little Cressingham, near Swaffham, and had been told there was a lot of 'bad blood' between the village and its neighbour, Great Cressingham.

'I was told that was all due to them being on different sides in "the war".

' "Which war?," I asked.

'He replied, as though the question was quite unnecessary, "The Civil War!"'

When you think the English Civil War was in the 1640s - more than 350 years ago! - that's an amazing story.

Or is it?

This chapter looks at some more of the unexpected ways in which this bloody period of British history has echoed down the years in Norfolk - in folklore and in fact.

War and peace
When Oliver Cromwell and his Roundheads beat Charles I - and chopped off his head - in the biggest upset in British history, it was the first (and only) time that we haven't been ruled by a king or queen.

For many people it must have seemed that the world had turned completely upside down.

Apart from Kett's Rebellion in 1549 (and the Romans' revenge after Boudica's defeat almost 2,000 years ago) this was the only time that Norfolk found itself caught up in serious civil strife.

We've see in 'NASTY NORFOLK' how King's Lynn tried to hold out against the Roundhead troops, who ended up winning a siege. And in 'NASTY NORWICH' we've heard about the explosive Royalist riots in Norwich.

But although the Siege of Lynn was the closest Norfolk got to a big battle, there must have been other, smaller, disputes.

There's lots of stories, for example, of Cromwell's troops taking over churches for use as stables.

Yes, that's right - stables.

He and his supporters followed a form of Christianity which they believed was 'purer' than anyone else's (which is why they were called 'Puritans'). They wanted to sweep away anything that got in the way - decoration in church, carvings, stained glass, you name it.

The sight of soldiers going round smashing up things must have been truly shocking. You weren't going to forget that if you saw it. And in at least three cases it's possible that people did remember, even hundreds of years later...

Musket memories

In 'NASTY NORWICH' we tell the story of one of those Civil War 'souvenirs', the musket ball left lodged in the top of a tomb in Norwich Cathedral by one of the Roundhead soldiers who'd burst in and started shooting.

And we know of two more examples, both from Norfolk villages.

At South Creake there was a village tradition that Cromwell's soldiers had forced their way into the church and taken pot-shots at the church's beautiful wooden angels in the roof.

When the church roof was being repaired in the 1950s, the restorers took a close look at the angels.... and found musket balls still stuck in them.

Some people (spoilsports) say the damage was

'Hmm... so how come you're so sure the Roundheads came to this church?'

caused by churchwardens shooting at jackdaws and sparrows in the 18th century... but we rather like the Cromwell story, don't you?

And a similar thing happened at Worstead church, also in the 1950s. When the cover for the font was being restored, the restorers found lead shot - where the Roundheads had shot at the carvings on it.

With the tradition of Cromwell stabling his horses at such varied sites as the Red Mount Chapel in Lynn and the Church of St Mary the Less at Thetford, perhaps there's even more of 'Orrible Oliver's handiwork to be discovered.

Haunting history

With so many traditions about the Civil War being handed down through the generations, you won't be surprised it's been the source of some ghostly visitations too!

In 1955 a man was working in a Great Yarmouth building 'with Cromwellian associations' when he was confronted by a cavalier, who advanced on him with a drawn sword. The man pushed a broom through the spook - and ran!

That building wasn't named, but sounds like it could have been the Elizabethan House Museum on South Quay.

We've heard in 'NASTY NORFOLK' about the tradition that a room was used by the Roundheads when they were deciding what to do with the captured king.

There's another tradition that the ghosts of Cromwell and co can be seen, arguing all over again about what to do with the doomed king...

Another Royalist ghost was spotted in a North Norfolk manor house. A French nobleman was renting the house - whose location wasn't revealed - and had seen a Royalist and his lady walking through the hall and up the staircase in the early hours.

And the ghost said to flit among the avenue of trees next to Swaffham parish church may have some link with the period too.

There's a stronger connection, though, in our final story. The famous Black Boys pub in Aylsham market place used to be owned during the Civil War by Richard Andrews. He was reputed to have been killed by Cromwell's men and buried in the grounds... and his ghost came back to haunt it.

Royal tales

While we're on the subject of monarchs (and their fates),
let's hear some of the stories - historical and in folklore - of
Norfolk's royal links.

Luckless lovers

It's always a risky thing to be the lover of a king or queen -
and it's just as risky to be the person who gets in the way.

Here's two tales which show you why.

Henry VIII (and you know where this is going to end up
already, don't you?) had a wife called Catherine Howard.
Now, when she was younger, Catherine had been in love with
a young nobleman called Francis Dereham.

Francis might have been a bit
older by now. But he certainly
wasn't any wiser. He made the
mistake of writing down in letters
about the relationship. The letters
fell into the hands of Henry's man
Thomas Cranmer in 1541.

*'You may think the
next bit is a slice of
bad luck too...'*

Poor Francis was soon
condemned to a horrible death - to
be hanged until almost dead, cut
down, disembowelled, cut in quarters
and then beheaded (just to make
sure).

There's a tradition that on its
way back to West Dereham, his
head got lost from the rest of his
body. And so the ghost of Francis
walks the grounds of the old abbey,
searching, searching...

Another Royal love-story-gone-wrong came later in the Tudor era. Amy Robsart was the daughter of Sir John Robsart of Syderstone Hall, and also had family links with Rainthorpe Hall and Stanfield (near Wymondham).

In 1550 she married the dashing young nobleman Robert Dudley. But when Queen Elizabeth came to the throne in 1558, Robert soon made himself a big favourite at court.

'I'm "stairing" at a nasty fate...'

While Amy stayed at home, Dudley became closer and closer to the queen.

Then, in September 1560, while Amy was staying at Cumnor Hall in Oxfordshire, she was found at the bottom of the stairs - with a broken neck.

Did she fall - or was she pushed? Rumours were rife across the country that poor Amy had been got rid of so that Dudley could marry the queen (in the end, he didn't, but stayed a favourite for almost 30 years).

There's a famous painting by W F Yeames which shows Amy at the bottom of the stairs with a couple of shadowy figures looking on. Her murderers?

And you won't be surprise to hear that the ghost of Amy is reputed to have haunted both Syderstone Hall (where she is dressed in her finest Tudor clothes) and also Rainthorpe Hall...

And here's another funny thing. One of her descendants

was Dorothy Walpole. Yes *that* Dorothy - the Brown Lady of Raynham Hall.

Two ghosts in one family. Now that's greedy...

A tale of three queens...

Talking of Elizabeth, there's a tradition that she hid in the tower of Shelton church to escape from her half-sister Mary (who was always trying to find out if Elizabeth was plotting against her).

And, funnily enough, there's a Norfolk link with Mary too. She was staying at the now-vanished Kenninghall Palace, belonging to the Duke of Norfolk, when she heard about her half-brother Edward's death in 1553 and ordered messages to be sent to London to have her declared queen.

Another famous Norfolk queenly link was over at Castle Rising castle hundreds of years before.

Queen Isabella was strongly suspected of having taking part in the murder of her husband Edward II.

When her son became Edward III he executed her lover and banished her to the Norfolk castle. Her ghost is supposed to haunt the castle, screaming as she goes.

But history shows that she was kept in good conditions and went on visits. Isabella eventually became a nun and died in 1358.

...er, and another one

Well, sort of.

Ever head of Queen Martha of England? No?

Well, she wasn't really a queen, but she certainly thought she was. Martha Stanninot (or Staninought - no-one was quite sure) of Great Yarmouth (who died in 1804 aged 70) used to live in one of its famous rows and became convinced that she was really royalty.

So she used to walk to Norwich sometimes to call on 'her' Bishop of Norwich.

Once she even went to London - walking all the way - to see the Prime Minister.

Now, if you turned up on the doorstep of 10 Downing Street nowadays claiming to be the queen, chances are you'd get some very odd looks - and be hurried away by a couple of very burly policemen.

But the PMs must have been a bit more approachable in the 18th century, as Martha was promised by him that the 'next cart-full of money which should come into the town was for her'.

The Yarmouth councillors ended up giving the eccentric Martha an allowance so she had enough to live on - which, of course, she took as being tribute from her grateful subjects!

Tales of Treasure

Losers...

For hundreds - even thousands of years - people have been finding treasure in Norfolk. And losing it.

Remember the story of King John we mentioned briefly in 'NASTY NORFOLK'?

The full story is a fascinating one. The rotten king was being chased around the country when his troops tried to cross the treacherous tidal waters of the Wash in October 1216.

One chronicler wrote that 'bottom-less whirlpools engulfed everything, together with men and horses, so that not a single foot-soldier got away to bear tidings of the disaster to the king'.

A list of John's treasure was made only a few months before the disaster, and by comparing that with what was left when Henry III was crowned a few years later, we can guess that the lost items included the imperial crown of Germany.

If the story is true - and some historians have cast doubt on it - the treasure will be buried under metres of soil and be well inland, because over the centuries great chunks of the Wash have been drained of water and turned into farmland.

Something clearly happened to the royal treasure – but what?

Some people think John secretly sold some of the treasure to pay for his wars - or that when he died a few days later at Newark, all his stuff was pinched (the Abbot of Croxton even took away his *intestines* as a souvenir*).

That's a really famous story. But did you know there was ANOTHER king who lost his money crossing the Wash - exactly 254 years to the month later?

Yes, really. It happened during the civil wars known as the Wars of the Roses, when a succession of nobles from northern England tried to grab the throne off each other.

When Edward IV found himself in trouble in October 1470, he rushed across the country with the Duke of Gloucester (the future Richard III) to try to escape.

When they reached King's Lynn and set off to Holland (and safety), the king had to give the ship's captain his own fur coat as payment - because they had lost their money on the way, and the lives of some of their soldiers.

*(*That took some guts...)*

...and finders

There are lots of tales of treasures being found in Norfolk, some true and some just stories.

Like the story of the Silver Well at Shouldham, where a similar story is told to the one about the Callow Pit at Moulton St Mary (see 'NASTY NORFOLK'). A treasure box was discovered and was being pulled out until someone unwisely suggested the Devil himself couldn't stop them getting rich.

Bad idea. The box was pulled back down... all the way to Hell.

Other stories were told about ponds near Dereham and about a field just outside Colkirk.

The Colkirk field had an area known as 'Drake North', which is a version of 'Dragon's Hoard' - people often spoke of buried treasure being guarded by dragons in Viking times.

Meanwhile in Great Yarmouth one of its Rows was called 'Money Office Row' and inspired a tradition that a box of treasure was buried there but as soon as it was dug up, it would vanish.

And at Lyng, there is a hill called 'Hogback', covering the ruins of St Edmund's Chapel. A legend says a drain runs under the chapel, and one day two boatmen found their way in it and discovered the silver chalice of the chapel (a special cup used in services).

They had a row about it and one used a 'terrible oath' (swore) - at which point the chalice jumped up in the air and buried itself back into the water. It was never seen again.

In the 16th century a former monk of St Benet's Abbey, William Stapleton, reckoned he could cast a spell to raise the spirit of buried treasure at various places in the county, including Syderstone, Norwich and Walsingham.

He failed.

And was jailed.

One of the places he tried to find treasure was Creake Abbey. Hundreds of years later, someone else tried to discover the same thing.

The decade? The 1950s.

'I'm a solid-gold failure!'

The searcher? Ian Fleming - creator of James Bond.

He didn't find anything either. Which was a shame, because what a great story he would have made of that!

Devilishly bad

We've mentioned the Devil a couple of times already. You can't have a good story without a terrific 'baddie' - and let's face it, you can't find a worse 'baddie' than him. Norfolk has tons of tales... let's sample a few, shall we?

Putrid place-names

The Devil popped up all over Norfolk, if place names are anything to go by. There's a Devil's Hole between Cockthorpe and Stiffkey, where the earth always stays dry because of an awful crime committed there.

Or try these: Devil's Bottom at East Winch, Devil's Plantation at Kelling, Devil's Hole - again - this time at Woodbastwick, and Devil's Dykes. The sea next to Cromer was known as 'the Devil's Throat'

'1...2...3...4... - Someone's going to get a Devil of a surprise!'

because of the terrible dangers to ships when a north wind was blowing.

And local legend has it that Thetford Castle Mound was created by the Devil scraping his boots after digging out Devil's Dyke. There's a hollow in the ground to the north east of the castle called 'the Devil's Hole'.

Apparently, if you walk round it seven times at midnight, you'll see its owner!

Beating Beelzebub

You had to be very smart - or very holy - to outwit Satan.

Once upon a time there was a young monk of St Benet's Abbey who became fed up with the quiet and dutiful life and ran away to go drinking, gambling and chasing after young women instead.

'Ah-ha,' thought the Devil, 'Here's someone I can carry off back to Hell!'

But luckily for the young monk, at that very moment St Benet himself re-appeared - and fought the Devil until he decided he just couldn't beat the saint and vanished in a puff of sulphur.

Sir Barnabas Brograve of Worstead used his brain, not his battling skills, to beat the Devil.

Sir Barnabas once boasted to his mowers that he could beat anyone at cutting down the crops at harvest - even the Devil himself.

So, of course, Satan duly appeared and refused to let Sir B get out of his bet.

Two acres of beans were set aside for the contest, but cunning Sir Barnabas had hidden some thin iron rods in the Devil's field.

As the Devil kept stopping to sharpen his scythe, he said to his opponent: 'I say, Barney bor, them bunks [thistles] do cut damned hard...'

The Wicked Squire of Woodbastwick

Of course, the Devil wasn't always beaten. Take the case of Colonel Thomas Sidney (or Sedley), who lived at Woodbastwick Old Hall. He was a hard-drinking, wife-beating bully - and had even whipped the vicar for daring to criticise him for going hunting on a Sunday.

In December 1770 he had a bet that his horse could win a race from the Rising Sun pub at Coltishall to Hoveton St John.

He was about to lose the race when he cheated big-time - by shooting the other person's horse!

That night, he was being served his evening meal when a dark stranger burst in, seized him by the throat and chucked him over his horse, which then galloped out of the hall grounds and plunged - producing clouds of steam - into Ranworth Broad.

Wicked Colonel S is doomed to appear every December 31, riding round the broad with his pack of ghostly hounds.

Spring-Heeled Jack

One of the strangest stories people used to tell until well into the last century, was the tale of 'Spring-Heeled Jack', a modern version of the Devil.

He was reported from all over the country - a mysterious, dark and very tall stranger who would jump in giant leaps to frighten his victims, laughing horribly all the time.

He was said to have

'Er... that wasn't your stomach going BOING, was it dear?'

appeared in Norwich in 1858 (see 'NASTY NORWICH') but he also popped up in Little Melton Lane (now Rectory Lane), between Attleborough and Shropham, at North Walsham, and possibly back in Norwich as the creature known as the 'Gildencroft Bogeyman'.

The bogeyman had saucer-eyes - *very* big and *very* scary. And that's enough to make anyone jump.

The Tale of Devil's Alley

This alley runs between Nelson Street and the South Quay at King's Lynn. It's easy to imagine on a dark night, with the waves lapping in the distance and no street lights, that this would have been a spooky place.

Sometime in the late 19th century, a man was drinking in a pub nearby when he was told how a murder had been committed in that very alley on Christmas Eve.

The killer had never been caught, and old folk swore it was the Devil who had done the evil deed, because every Christmas Eve there were screams and devilish laughter.

Being Christmas Eve, the man decided to see if the story were true. So he joined forces with another couple of people in the pub and persuaded them to walk down the alley from the Nelson Street side, while he travelled from the quayside.

'Huh, he's the REAL scaredy cat here!'

While he was carefully walking up the dark alley he suddenly noticed saucer-like eyes and a strange sound.

He collapsed to the ground with shock and was found a couple of minutes later by the other group...

...with the alley cat whose eyes had so scared him, just slipping away into the night and wondering what all the fuss was about!

Nasty Nuns, Putrid Priests and Vile Vicars

There's something about churches, abbeys and the like which inspire many great tales of the supernatural. Perhaps it's because it's easy to conjure up thoughts of creepy things when you think about churchyards and a dark night, with the wind rustling in the trees and....

Gulp. Hang on while I fetch my comfort blanket.

Ah, that's better. Now for some more scary stories...

The Gateley Ghost
This story happened in the little village of Gateley, which is near North Elmham.

On December 12 1706, Robert Withers, the vicar, recorded the story of a Mr Shaw who was sitting in his study between 11pm and midnight when his old friend Mr Naylor walked in.

'How nice,' I hear you say. 'Fancy his friend coming over to see him - a bit late in the evening though.'

Er, 'late' is definitely the right word. For Mr Naylor had been *dead* for four years.

Mr Shaw said: 'When I saw him I was not much affright-ed, and I asked him to sit down, which accordingly he did for two hours and we talked together.

'He said "Mr Orchard [another friend] will be with me soon, and yourself not long after!".'

He was right. Mr Orchard and Mr Shaw both died very soon after that...

The Exorcist's House

This old house over-looks the churchyard of St Nicholas' Chapel at King's Lynn. It is right in the middle of the old fishermen's quarter of the town, and gets its name from the belief that its former residents  included a priest who made his living by chasing off ghosts and spirits from people's houses.

Local fishermen reckoned the house was haunted ('Something happens every Halloween', they used to say), and a 15-year-old girl in the 1970s was surprised to see an old lady sitting in a rocking chair by the fire.

Or rather, the ghost of an old lady...

Putrid Priests

The village of Sturston, near Stanford in Breckland, was regarded as a cursed village. It had a field called Hangman's Round - the village parson (who was also the local squire) hanged himself from the branch of an oak tree there. In March 1550 a witch had cursed the squire (Sir Miles Yare) and the whole village.

And another priest features in a story about the Maddermarket Theatre in Norwich. The Eastern Evening News reported in December 1953 how the ghost of a Roman Catholic priest had been spotted (and vanished) during a Saturday show at the theatre sometime in the 1920s.

The building was a Catholic church from the end of the 18th century and some people have claimed they can some-times smell incense - the spicy perfume burned during services.

Another Catholic priest is said to have haunted Bury Hall at Ashill since at least the 1930s. The ghost is the spirit of a priest who was found hiding at the hall in the 16th century and killed by Protestant investigators.

The ghostly priest used to turn up around 3am, usually in the run-up to Easter, and made his presence felt by banging doors and tearing off bedclothes.

Vile Vicarages

There was something not quite right in the vicarage of All Saints' Church in the area then known as South Lynn (which has moved further out of the town over the years).

One of the rooms was reputed to be haunted.

In 1825 John Greaves, then aged 14 or 15, decided to investigate. He had heard lots of strange noises, which he blamed on rats scurrying around.

But by tapping on the walls he discovered one was hollow. He made a hole in the brickwork and found - a skeleton, dressed in a bride's outfit.

This story has definite echoes of another famous one - known as the 'Mistletoe Bough' - told about Lovell's Hall in Terrington St Clement and Brockdish Hall near Diss. It goes like this: on her wedding day a bride and groom and their guests decide to play  a game of hide-and-seek. The bride goes into the dustiest attic room she can find, where she discovers an old trunk.

She opens up the lid and hides inside. But when it comes to getting out, she finds the lid has stuck.

She bangs and screams to be let out. But no-one can hear her.

Frantically, the groom and the guests search for the bride but she has vanished. Then, many years later, the husband - now an old man - is sorting out an attic room when he comes across an old chest and... well, you can guess the rest.

The Hethersett Haunting

In February 1900 the wife of the Rev Charles Tweedale, who was just about to start his duties in the village, was shocked to see a man coming down the stairs wearing an old-style cassock [priest's robe].

The man was identical to the one in a painting of a Dr Caius which hung at the top of the stairs. The reverend took down the picture and locked it away in the attic.

But two days later, Dr Caius was back - and soon bells started ringing around the house. This went on for two months, even though the wires which pulled the bells had been cut.

The haunting ended with spooky footsteps, thumping noises and all the bells ringing round the house at once. A new servant who had just arrived in the house was so scared she snatched up her own wet clothes from the wash tub and ran out of the house.

Never to come back.

Mouldering Monks

There's only a tiny bit left of the once-mighty St Benet's Abbey in the Broads. But look closely at the arch on a moonlight night and you may see the ghostly form of a monk, swinging on the end of a rope.

This was the traitor who had let the Norman soldiers sneak into the abbey soon after the 1066 invasion. His reward was death.

A famous ghostly monk story happened in May 1937, when their ghostly chanting was heard in the house known as The Canons, alongside Thetford Priory. The residents had apparently heard the sound of a complete service (in Latin) and the noise made by the monks' sandals on the stone floor.

Another monk - but a faceless one - was remembered by a Great Yarmouth woman in 1972. She used to live in a house which overlooked the site of the new fire station at Friars Lane.

She remember that she had seen the mugless monk when she was a little girl - and an old woman in a black frock, plus a girl with golden hair. The hauntings happened around midnight, preceded by the sound of eerie whistling....

'Let's face it, I'm scary'

More monks were blamed for the curse which was supposed to affect land behind the Lynn County Court building by The Walks. The tower of a workhouse on the site collapsed in the 19th century, a cinema and dance hall built there burned down, and the storeroom of a scenic artist was reputedly haunted.

48

Three monks were also supposed to haunt a room at the old Samson and Hercules ballroom overlooking Tombland in Norwich.

And a spooky modern story happened in 1966, when Anglia television showed a programme called 'Look At East Anglia', which included a piece about Old Morley Hall. Twenty-three viewers wrote in to say they had seen the figure of a bearded monk looking out of one of the windows...

Nasty Nuns

Although spooky monks seem to be the most popular, ghostly nuns have their share of stories too.

The ghost of one is supposed to be seen sometimes gliding across Priory Plain in Great Yarmouth, heading for the churchyard.

And over at Prince of Wales Road in Norwich, the Mann Egerton garage (now redeveloped) - on the site of the old Greyfriars - had a nun who put in an appearance three times in the 1959-60 period alone.

The nun was said to be dressed in black or grey, with a white headdress and black shoes. Just before she appeared everything suddenly went very cold...

Chairs - and scares

A former Norwich rector was renting an old house in St Martin-at-Palace Plain (near the cathedral).

But whenever he sat down in a particular room to study or write a sermon he had the strangest feeling that someone - or *something* - was standing behind his chair. And visitors to the house reported having exactly the same feeling in the room.

Eventually the study floor was taken up during renovations to the house - and there was the skeleton of a woman. The hauntings stopped when the skeleton was buried in a proper churchyard.

There was another disturbing experience in a house in the Chantry. A bright light was seen shining under one of the doors. But as soon as the door was opened, the light stopped...

The White Lady of Worstead

Worstead church is said to be haunted by this particular spirit, who shows herself at midnight on Christmas Eve (presumably checking to see if Father Christmas has been).

One day - some say in 1830 - a villager boasted that he would stay in the church to ring a bell at midnight.

When midnight came and went, his friends rushed into the church - and found the terrified man saying 'I've seen her! I've seen her!', then dropping down stone dead.

Terrifying Tunnels

We heard in 'NASTY NORFOLK' about the story of the fiddle-player who offered to explore the tunnel which ran from Red Mount Chapel in King's Lynn to Castle Rising castle - and vanished forever.

There are loads of similar tales from all over Norfolk.

A monk is said to haunt another tunnel, which runs from the old Magdalen Priory to St Peter's Church at Wiggenhall St Peter.

Perhaps the oldest tunnels are the ones supposed to link the Roman town at Caistor St Edmund with Arminghall Church, and then there's the Iron Age earthwork at Warham, near Wells.

In fact, these tunnels almost always end (or begin) in an old church or priory. Like between Bury Hall at Ashill and Holme Hale church, and Ranworth Church and St Benet's Abbey.

The tunnel supposed to run between Binham Priory and Walsingham Abbey has its own ghost stories.

A tall figure dressed in black is supposed to walk along the path of the tunnel - and there's a version of the story of the fiddler told about this one too. With one twist: in the 1930s council workmen were digging at the site of 'Fiddler's Hill' - where the violinist had vanished - when they found the skeletons of a man and his dog. Or so the story goes!

In Norwich there was supposed to be a link between the old Mile Cross and St Faith's Priory, and also one between the Castle, Cathedral, St Andrew's Hall and a building in Cathedral Close. The cathedral was also supposed to have been linked to the Maid's Head Hotel by a passage once used - so the Victorian rumour had it - to brick up nuns until they starved to death...

So what's the real story behind all these tales? The passages seem to have been drains or cellars.

Monasteries often had very posh loos (well, by comparison with the stinking horrible places other people had to put up with anyway), called 'rere-dorters' where running water carried away the monks' poo.

When you peer into one and all you can see is dark - well, it's easy to think it goes on for miles.

'Scary tunnels? Try going down to our loos!'

And the 'smugglers' tunnels' found at Wells usually turned out to be sewers too.

Oh, and that Red Mount Chapel story might have had a simple explanation after all. In the 19th century a Lynn historian found the doorway. But when he explored he found that after a few feet he came to a dead end - and not a dead fiddler.

Rum Religion

We've already met some ghostly (and ghastly) nuns, monks and vicars. But the world of religion has some more strange corners...

An Appetite for Marriage

People get married for all sorts of reasons, but mostly because they love each other, of course (either that or they can't find anyone else to put up with the smell of their socks).

But one Norfolk vicar married for another reason: because he was *hungry!*

The Rev John Beevor took over Scarning parish in November 1789 and for ten years he lived there quite happily, mainly because his long-suffering wife and their cook made lots of food to satisfy his greedy appetite.

But then in April 1799 his wife died. John came back from the funeral service sad, tearful... and very

hungry. He looked in all the cupboards. No food. So he went to the village pub.

The next day he was even hungrier, only for the cook to tell him that she was leaving her job.

The parson begged her to stay. So she did... on one condition: That he married her. Which he did.

But Parson Beevor (and his stomach) didn't live happily ever after. The villagers didn't like the way the ex-servant swanned round the place like she had been born really posh.

So they chased her (and him) out of the village for good...

Scary Sparrow

Not the bird, but the Bishop of Norwich - the Rt Rev Anthony Sparrow. In 1678 he received a letter which had him hiding behind the sofa in terror.

It read: 'Your days are very short and narrow, your proceedings very sharp, I will kill you... it seems you are grown a viper not fit to live. You limb of Satan, farewell'.

Bishop Sparrow passed it to the Lord Lieutenant of Norfolk, who sent it to the king. The government used it as an excuse to imprison six people for years (one was called Cromwell, funnily enough).

One of the six spent three years in jail without being charged with any-thing. As a souvenir of his stay he caught scurvy (where all your teeth drop out), asthma (when some-times you can hardly breathe) and dropsy (where horrible fluid starts gathering in your body). Nice.

'Prison is a right pain in the gum!'

Rotten Relics

We've come across some strange examples of this in 'NASTY NORFOLK'. Basically, churches and monasteries in the Middle Ages used to compete to have supposedly holy treasures which they could then use to attract people to come to visit - and spend their lovely cash.

Relics were usually saintly body bits (the head of John the Baptist, for example).

Over at Thetford, the church of St Audrey claimed to have her smock - and if you worshipped it and were very good (and made a donation, naturally) it would cure your toothache and sore throat.

It could also do big miracles too. One day William and Isabelle Heddrich of Hockham took their three-year-old daughter with them when they went to help with the harvest.

The little girl went to sleep at the edge of the field - but a cart which was travelling past accidentally ran over her head and killed her.

Her grieving parents prayed to St Audrey to bring their daughter back to life. If she did, they promised, they would walk to Thetford to her shrine - without any clothes on.

At midnight, the child woke up.

And the parents? They kept to their vow and walked the 15 miles to Thetford completely and utterly naked. I

'So whose idea was it to take a short cut through the nettle patch?'

know, it's 'barely' believable, isn't it?

The Cursed Cross

When the abbey at Langley was closed on the orders of Henry VIII, its cross was kept by the village. A tradition said that if it were ever moved again, Langley Hall would catch fire the very same day.

But they didn't listen, did they? Because, yes, they moved it and, yes, the hall caught fire...

Calamitous Christening

Churches were always having rows about things in the Middle Ages. St Margaret's Church (or rather, Priory as it was then) in King's Lynn was keen to stay the most important church in the town. So when St Nicholas' Chapel in the North End of Lynn asked for permission to baptise children, St Maggie's said a very un-Christian 'Get lost!'.

So St Nick's went to the biggest cheese of them all - the Pope - and asked him instead. He said 'yes' in 1378.

But St Margaret's still said 'no'.

St Nicholas' Chapel tried again. And again. And again.

It took almost 250 years to get St Margaret's to finally agree to let the chapel do Christenings. In 1627 the first baby was baptised (at last) in St Nicholas' Chapel.

Happy ending? Not quite - it died just 24 days later.

Wymondham Wrangle

Wymondham Abbey is one of Norfolk's most famous buildings, and celebrated its 900th anniversary in 2007. But it's also rather strange - because it has a tower at both ends!

And it all happened because of - you've guessed it - another huge row. When the abbey was built, its founder, William D'Albini, thought it would be a really, really clever thing to have part for the monks and part for the townsfolk.

In fact it turned out to be a really, really stupid thing, as for the next hundred or so years the two sides argued and fought over the place. Eventually (1249), the row was sent to the Pope to sort out.

The abbey originally had two towers at one end and other big one in the middle. The Pope decided the parish should have one of the double-towers and the north bit of the abbey, and the monks the rest.

Sorted.

Er, not quite.

Round Two began when the big tower in the middle had to

be pulled down 150 years or so later. The monks built another (it's the one you can see at the east end today), put their bells in it - and built a big wall to stop the townsfolk using them.

The row got heated - in fact, it was a right ding-dong*. The king (Henry IV) had to send England's top churchman, the Archbishop of Canterbury, to sort out the dispute.

After 20 years of arguing, the townsfolk put up their own tower and bells to replace the old double-towers. That's the tower you can see at the west end today. But they had to agree not to ring it when it might disturb the monks - not after 6pm or before 6am.

'Look, I know we shouldn't disturb the monks, but this is ridiculous!'

It was the end of the rows.

But history had a nasty footnote lined up for the new west tower. After Wymondham landowner Robert Kett's bloody and unsuccessful rebellion in 1549, he was hanged from Norwich Castle. But his brother was brought back home - and hanged from the west tower.

But whether his ghost still swings there on a dark and creepy night.... well, that's for a brave soul to find out.

And, no, we're not volunteering.

(*and that is, officially, the worst joke in this book)

More Ghastly Ghosts

And talking about spooks, it's about time we had another gruesome helping. We'll be looking at some of the stories told about the cruel countryside. Everything nice and sweet in those country lanes? Not when you read this chapter!

The Phantom from the Pit

Once there was a group of poachers who were out at night near Croxton - but the local gamekeeper discovered them. The poachers grabbed the poor gamekeeper and killed him to keep him quiet.

Or *thought* they had killed him.

As they were carrying his body back towards Thetford he suddenly revived near a pond called Chalk Pit. So the poachers had another go at killing him - and managed to do it properly this time. They buried the gamekeeper by the pit and ran away.

And on certain nights, a ghostly funeral carriage, complete with coffin and coffin-bearers comes out of the pit to frighten unwary passers-by...

The Fork Frightener

Sometime in the 1850s or 1860s - so another story goes - there was a farmer who lived beside the old King's Lynn to Wisbech road, near Tilney All Saints.

One day he went into his barn - and a few moments later a terrible scream was heard.

When the sound was investigated, there was a horrible sight - the farmer was found dead with his pitchfork sticking in his neck. Since then, the place has been haunted by his never-resting ghost...

Terrible Traveller

Round about the same time, a jeweller-watchmaker was walking from house to house in the Tittleshall and Wellingham area offering to sell his wares. Two farmworkers saw him walking - alone - along the lonely road which runs between the villages... and that was the last time he was seen alive.

'Take it as red, there's something nasty in that wood...'

Soon after, someone noticed some blood near a small wood and followed the trail until he discovered the murdered man in a ditch. The culprit was soon found - and hanged.

And ever since then, the ghost of the jeweller - complete with bloodstains - walks near the wood.

And talking about trees, here's a couple more creepy tales.

At Great Melton, an old beech tree in the area known as 'Coldblow Hill' - by the Norwich-Watton road - was supposed to have the ghost of a woman who rocks her baby to sleep at midnight.

Over at Stratton St Mary, a Parson Solley had to hold a special service to try to keep a ghost trapped in an oak forever.

The Housekeeper Who Wasn't

Farmer and writer Lucilla Reeve often claimed she could see strange things. Like the time she arrived at her farm at Bagmore, near Stanford, and looked up to see her house-keeper, Harriet, peering out of an upstairs window.

Lucilla shouted up to Harriet about her making some supper (it was 11pm) - the housekeeper smiled but said nothing.

Miss Reeve went inside, discovered Harriet hadn't come downstairs, so ended up making her own supper.

She mentioned it to the housekeeper next morning. But Harriet said she had never been out of bed - or even awake...

Haunted Heath

Massingham Heath, which runs between Great Massingham and Grimston, is a lonely spot even today, so it's easy to see how ghosts were sometimes never far from people's minds.

Once a man and his wife were crossing it in a carriage when they heard a scream which sounded like an animal caught in a trap. They stopped and the woman got out to look for the poor creature.

But then there was a scream from another direction - then another. The wife hurried back into the carriage only for more screams to sound from right under the wheels.

The horses, terrified, set off at a gallop.

Later - much later - when the couple were back at home they discovered that two travellers had once been murdered on the lonely heath...

Cruel Cures, Pathetic Prophecies and Silly Superstitions

The countryside wasn't just full of ghost stories - it was full of lots of other scary things too. Like what happened if you fell ill...

Cruel Cures

For hundreds - thousands - of years, the only way people could make themselves better if they were sick was:

I Hope,

II Consult the nearest witch (and more about that in the next chapter) or...

III Try one of the zillions of countryside cures.

We're already met some of these in 'NASTY NORFOLK' (snail slime, moles' blood and fried mice included), but there were plenty more 'cures' which sounded worse than the disease.

If you caught typhoid fever (common in the days when people's water supplies were full of poo and germs) then the country cure was to put one of the gooey inside bits of a cow - its spleen - on the bottom of your feet.

If you had just had a common-or-garden fever, then the spleen of a sheep would do instead.

'The doctor's say it's the best cure, baaa none!'

Whooping with joy. Sort of.
Whooping cough was a very common disease, especially of young children. But happily there were three great cures. Yes, really.

Er, no really, actually. Cure number one: put a live flat fish on your chest until it died.

Cure number two: Drink some milk which has been shared with... a ferret.

But cure number three was a bit more complicated: you had to dig a hole in a meadow, put the sick child into it - head first - then put the grass and earth you'd just dug up on to its head. When the child coughed, it would be better.

If it hadn't choked to death on all the soil first, of course.

Midnight malaria
People who lived in marshy areas such as the Broads or the Fens used to catch malaria ('ague') from mosquitoes. Getting rid of it involved a clock, a nail - and a passer-by.

It went like this.

Begin by going a crossroads alone.

As the church clock strikes midnight... BONG... turn round three times... BONG... hit a nail down into the ground... BONG...and walk away backwards... BONG... before the clock stops striking... BONG...

If you do this according to the instructions, then the next person who walks past the nail will catch your malaria instead - leaving you healthy.

Dead impressive cures

If you kept getting cramp - sharp pains in your muscles – then all you had to do was put a ring on your finger.

So what could possibly be nasty about that? Er, the rings had to be made out of coffin handles.

'That should cure your "coffin!"!'

It got even worse if you wanted to get rid of 'fleshy excrescences' - lumps and bumps on your body. You had to pass the hand of a dead body over the bump for three days in a row...

Chambers of horrors

By the end of the 18th century there were lots of 'quack doctors' popping up in towns who would offer to sell you a bottle of some wonder potion to cure your disease. Did the potions work?

Take a look at a couple of recipes from Dereham doctor Dr John Chambers' book of herbal remedies from 1800, and make up your own minds.

Viper broth (=snake soup): 'Take a very young lean chicken, skin it, and boil it with three parts of water. Skim it well and put in a dried viper cut in pieces'.

Drink a large cupful two to three times a day, and you'd ssssssoon feel better....

Or try this one: snails and worms boiled in milk. Gather your snails ('as many as you please'), remove their shells and boil them with some milk until it makes a jelly.

Add a couple of sugary herbal mixtures.

And if you preferred the worm version, you have to wash the dirt off and cut them into three-centimetre pieces. 'After boiling in the same manner as above, you may add any sort of spice and sweeten to taste.'

Yum, yum.

If you don't fancy that then how about another great remedy from Dr Chambers' book... peacock poo.

Pathetic Prophecies

Norfolk has several strange rhymes handed down over hundreds of years.

The most famous - which we mentioned in 'NASTY NORWICH' was about the area of Norwich called Dussindale. Kett's rebels deliberately fought their last battle there because they believed the rhyme predicted they would win. It didn't - and neither did they.

Another famous one is 'He who would old England win/ Must at Weybourne Hoop begin'.

There's a very similar rhyme (about Scotland and England) quoted in Shakespeare's Henry V (written in 1598), so this Norfolk version could be at least as old.

It refers to the deep water which lies near there - in other words, an ideal place for enemy ships to come and land their armies.

And as for prophecies, there's another one supposed to have been said by the Yorkshire woman Mother Shipton hundreds of years ago about Lynn. It's said that she predicted Greyfriars Tower would fall down on a building full of people.

Since, happily, the beautiful medieval building has just been lovingly restored, that's one prediction which doesn't look as if it could be coming true for, oh, the next few hundred years - and hopefully, never.

Silly superstitions

Until the 1870s, there was no system of general education. People picked up what knowledge they could gather from their families or friends. Sometimes they could be really, really ignorant of what Norfolk people still call 'book larnin''

Lynn fisherman Frank Castleton recalled that when he was a young boy (he was born in 1903) there were some of the old boatmen who believed that the world was flat - or that there was a different sun and moon every day.

'It was all pebbles round here when I was a lad!'

And, elsewhere, some country people believed that stones grew in the fields.

That's not to say these farmworkers or fishermen were stupid - like thousands of other people, they had never been to school (or only very briefly).

They had to go out and earn money instead, to help their families as soon as possible.

So people relied a lot on superstitions and sayings to guide them through life.

There were hundreds of them in Norfolk. Most have been lost, but luckily some Victorian historians realised they were worth writing down.

Here's a few of them...

Heard a cuckoo calling? That's nice - but not if you were in bed at the time.

That meant that you (or one of your friends) were going to die soon. If you were walking when you heard it, however, then that was lucky.

There were several superstitions about Good Friday, the day when Jesus was nailed to the Cross. It was considered very unlucky to wash on that day, because there was a tradition that Christ had been given soapy water when he asked for a drink. But on the other hand, if you baked a cake on Good Friday, it would never go mouldy - a piece was great if you had diarrhoea (non-stop pooing).

If knives were crossed on your plate that meant a quarrel was likely.

Itches were useful guides too.

An itchy foot was a hint that you would be treading on strange ground soon.

An itchy right hand meant you would receive

= MONEY

= NO MONEY

= TRAVEL

= SOMEONE"S JUST FIRED AN ARROW THROUGH YOUR FOOT

money - but the opposite was true if your left hand itched.

If you cut a child's nails before it was 12 months old, then it would grow up to be a thief (you had to bite the nails off instead).

Things could be bad if you got outside your house too.

If you bumped into any red-haired men, beware - they were liars.

If you saw a cross-eyed man or woman on your journey that was bad luck - so you had to turn back. The same thing applied if you met a weasel.

And if you should be unlucky enough to meet a cross-eyed weasel with red hair, take our advice and run all the way home, lock the door, and hide under the duvet.

Oh, and take our advice – don't believe anything it tells you.

AAAARGH!!

'Was it something that I said?'

Woeful Witches

Witches - or the poor old ladies accused of being them - were a cause of much nastiness in Norfolk's story for hundreds of years. We've met some of them in 'NASTY NORWICH' and 'NASTY NORFOLK' - but there's plenty more to tell!

So sit down, make yourself comfortable and read for a spell.*

(*I was wrong. THIS is the worst joke.)

Making a splash

Near Harleston, there is a deep bit of the Waveney - one of the rivers that divides Norfolk from Suffolk - which used to be known as the 'Witch Pool'.

It got its name from the practice of 'floating witches'. If you were an old lady accused of being a witch you were wrapped in a sheet with your big toes and thumbs tied together.

You were then lowered into the pool. If you floated, you were guilty - and would be condemned to death. If you sank, you were innocent.

'OK, then, so she's innocent – fancy diving in to tell her?'

And probably dead by drowning.

And talking of water, if there was a disaster, people didn't blame nature if they could find someone to blame instead.

Records at Wells claimed that in 1583 Mother Gabley - 'a execrable [terrible] witch of Lynn' - had caused a shipwreck by boiling 'certeyne eggs in a payle full of colde water'. Thirteen men were lost in the disaster.

Bet that was the last time she had hard-boiled eggs for breakfast.

Fire... and fury

It wasn't just water that witches were said to influence. In 1613 a Margaret Byx confessed (under a bit of torture, no doubt) that she and an accomplice had raised a wind to stop a fire at Wymondham from being put out.

And a fiery temper was the undoing of Mary Smith of Lynn.

She was the wife of a glove-maker but made money for the family by selling cheese.

'All right, all right, I admit I raised the wind... but I blame it on the beans!'

Smith was really angry that other people were trying to make money the same way, so made an agreement with the Devil - and acquired a black cat.

She was eventually charged with murdering her neighbour John Orkney after he'd smacked her son.

Smith was executed in Tuesday Market Place in 1616. And the cat was probably tortured to death as its 'punishment'.

Talking of the Tuesday Market Place, its famous heart-shaped brick - which recalls the 1590 burning of another Lynn witch - is said to glow on certain nights...

Cunning plans

Those people claiming magical powers were known as 'cunning women' or 'cunning men' for centuries.

They could be helpful - *if* you paid them.

In the 19th century a man in a village near Great Yarmouth won some sausages in a raffle. But when he ate them he fell ill. His friends persuaded him to consult Mrs Mortimer, a cunning woman at Yarmouth.

'I said a bottle of wee, not a wee bottle!"

She gave him a copy of the Lord's Prayer to be worn next to his heart. And he had to send bits of his hair, toe-nail and finger-nail clippings (and a bottle of wee) so she could make her spell.

The man got better - so Mrs Mortimer demanded more money. When he refused, he got sick again... until he paid up.

Some cunning people could be even nastier. Mary Woods, known as 'Cunning Mary', was born near Norwich in the late 16th century.

She told people's fortunes and used her familiars (pets said to have been supplied by the Devil) to look for lost property or, more nastily, claim people were bewitched and offer to cure them... for a fee.

If the women (they were her usual clients) refused to pay up, Mary would threaten to tell everyone that they had asked her to poison their husbands.

She was whipped in 1612 for her horrible activities, and decided to move to London.

She ended up having to face questioning by the authorities after claiming that the Countess of Essex had left a diamond ring with her as part-payment for helping to murder her husband.

But perhaps Mary wasn't lying after all - because a few years later the (now-divorced) Countess of Essex was found guilty of poisoning Sir Thomas Overbury.

The American nightmare

There's a big Norfolk link to the most famous (or rather, notorious) witch trials of them all. Rebecca Towne was born in Yarmouth in the early 17th century but went over to the new colonies of America with her family.

She married a man called Francis Nurse and they lived happily in Salem, Massachusetts, until 1692, when some excitable girls accused her of being a witch. Poor Rebecca - who was in her seventies - tried to defend herself but she was found guilty and hanged.

Her sister Mary was also accused, found guilty and hanged.

A third sister, Sarah, was also accused but seems to have escaped after being transferred to the county jail.

Altogether 200 people were jailed in the witch scares, with 20 executed.

Amazingly, it took until 2001 - more than 300 years after the trials - for the Massachusetts State Governor to finally sign a law declaring that the last of the executed 'witches' were innocent.

Charming... and not so charming

Some people used charms as a sort of do-it-yourself witch-craft. One notorious Norfolk burglar had a Lord's Prayer written in reverse sewn into his waistband to supposedly protect him from being caught.

And in Upton, near Acle, in the 1870s there was still a belief that cow cream was sometimes bewitched - and the only certain cure was putting a red-hot poker into the top of the butter churn.

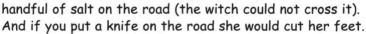

'I haven't the heart to do this!'

If you lived in the middle of Norfolk there were two guaranteed ways you could stop yourself being bewitched.

Method 1: Throw a handful of salt on the road (the witch could not cross it). And if you put a knife on the road she would cut her feet.

Method 2: Catch a mole, kill it and take out its heart before it has stopped beating. Urgghh. And then *eat* it. Double-urggh.

Er, I think I'll just be bewitched, if you don't mind.

Witch villages

There were certain places which had a reputation for having plenty of witches.

Bintree was reported to be 'riddled with reputed witches' in the 1840s, while South Walsham, too, was noted for its spell-casting inhabitants.

These included the nasty variety ('black' witches) and the not-quite-so-nasty ('white' witches - the 'cunning women').

There was even an old rhyme which went:

'Pahnser [Panxworth] dogs and Batswick [Woodbastwick] bitches,
Ranner [Ranworth] coots and Walsom witches.'

Terrible toads

We'll be taking a look at how the poor wildlife of Norfolk has been bashed, shot and generally mistreated in a later chapter.

But in the meantime we sign off this chapter on witches with a look at the fate of the toad. They were often accused of being 'familiars' of witches and so ended up being treated really badly.

Happily, these days we know the creatures are harmless amphibians which help clear our gardens of plant-scoffing creepy crawlies.

But back then, people just went 'YEEEEEEUCK!'.

Like the supposed spell for giving pain to something you didn't like, which involved grabbing a passing toad, giving it the name of your victim, sticking pins in it and - if that wasn't bad enough - shoving it up the chimney.

In fact if you wanted to become a witch you didn't have to pass Witch SATs or GCSEs.

'OK, OK - I get the point!'

All you needed was grab another passing toad - one of the species known as 'natterjack' this time - then pop it into an ants' nest.

When the ants had finished scoffing poor Nat, you had to put its skeleton into a stream and one bone would stay upright. It was owning this special bone which made you into a witch. Hmm.

But there is one toad story which we think is much scarier than any of those. Are you sitting comfortably? Then we'll begin.

Sometime in the early 19th century [this story was written down in 1877] in a 'village near Sheringham', a man called Joe Smith was helping an old lady and her son with the harvest on their small farm.

He was working in the field next to the farm when he looked across and saw his friend taking a snooze... with a large toad on his chest crawling towards his open mouth. Closer, closer....

Joe called out, and rushed over with his pitchfork. He knocked the toad off his friend and speared it with his pitchfork.

But a little while later the toad appeared again - with his insides hanging out - and crawling towards the son. Joe picked it up and threw it on the farmhouse fire.

The old lady picked it out of the fire and told him to chuck it in the pond instead.

But a few minutes later they were startled to see the toad, blackened with fire and covered with mud, crawling out of the pond, closer, closer....

And the old woman died very shortly after, which led some people to wonder if the toad had been a sort of vision of her death.

Either that, or the poor old toad just couldn't get the message that, no, these humans really, *really* didn't want to come out to play....

Dreadful Death and Foul Funerals

Foul fate

Death was never far away from the people of Norfolk for thousands of years.

Disease, violence, back-breaking work, polluted water and rotten food all combined to make the chance of a long life, oh, about the same as a giraffe doing the backstroke in your breakfast bowl of cornflakes.

Many of the superstitions we first talked about a couple of chapters ago were to do with death. For example, whoever watched in the church porch of Crostwick parish church on St Mark's Eve (April 25) would see the apparitions of those who were about to die.

A bird flying into a room, having a snake enter your house, or see-ing four crows sitting in a line, all meant that you would lose a relative.

'Looks like I've "adder" deadly visitor!'

Dead strange

If someone actually did peg out, there was a strange Norfolk superstition called the 'limp corpse'.

It was believed that if the body wasn't stiff very soon after death then it meant there would be another death within the year.

And digging the grave for our friendly dead person on a Sunday could be a very risky thing to do, as the superstition was that another one would then need to be dug within the same week.

The Norfolk historian Walter Rye, writing in 1872, recalled the story of a woman in an east Norfolk village who'd spotted a Sunday-dug grave.

'Ah!,' she said, 'There will be somebody else wanting a grave before the week is out!'

The prediction came true. For her.

Dead drunk

It used to be a custom at Norfolk funerals for vast amounts of booze to be drunk in honour of the dead person. Everyone who turned up for the funeral procession was given a piece of cake, beer and wine (so you can bet that *everyone* turned out for funerals), with the actual bearers of the coffin stuffed full of rum, gin or brandy.

One knight who was buried in the county had 48 bottles of wine drunk over his grave before the coffin was covered with earth. So, les jus' have a drink or two for the dead pershhhon. Hic!

Knock, knock...

Mind you, you'd have needed a drink after what happened at a funeral at Hoveton St Peter (now part of the main bit of Hoveton) around 1850.

A village girl died and was buried, but there were soon concerns that she hadn't really been dead.

The grave was frantically excavated, the lid taken off the coffin to find....

...that the 'corpse' had turned over.

Rest in pieces

Even when you were definitely, definitely dead and buried, you weren't allowed to rest in peace.

Well, not if you were Norwich's greatest-ever clever clogs, Sir Thomas Browne, anyway. He was buried in St Peter Mancroft church in 1682, dug up in 1840 and his skull sent to be an exhibit at the Norfolk and Norwich Hospital until 1922 - when Sir T finally got it back.

In the Norwich Gazette of April 1722 there was an advertisement from Robert Robinson of St Peter's parish offering 'a great choice of good second-hand coffins'. Did he face stiff competition, we wonder?

And in late 1815 the host of the Duke's Palace Inn in the city was puzzled by the late-night deliveries of apples to his stable which had been rented for two months by a fruit merchant.

'I thought these apples cost an arm and a leg... and I was right!'

One night the landlord peeped inside one of the sacks when no-one was around and found it full, not with apples, but a – gulp – *dead body*. It was the corpse of someone who had just been buried at Hainford.

The story was another of the notorious 'bodysnatching' cases we've met in 'NASTY NORWICH' and 'NASTY NORFOLK'.

People used to steal freshly-buried people and sell their bodies for cutting up by medical students.

All together now – YEEURCH!

Sad Suicides

If you took your own life - suicide - people were terrified that your spirit would come back to roam the earth. So the way they made sure your corpse stayed put under the ground was to fix it there... with a stake through the heart.

If you look at old maps of Norfolk you can often find crossroads (where suicides were traditionally buried) marked with names such as 'Pigg's Grave' and 'Bugg's Grave'. One Victorian writer even recorded that at a certain crossroads, roadworkers would always make sure to add a spadeful of earth to the burial mound.

This scary suicides belief explains a great story from Redenhall. A man called Lush was supposed to haunt a willow tree at a crossroads. The tree - called the 'Lush Bush' - was said to have grown from the stake driven into the dead man...

Grave mistakes

If you managed to survive being dropped by drunken coffin bearers, not dug up - or just been genuinely dead in the first place - then fate could still be waiting to rattle your bones.

At Great Yarmouth, some of the gravestones from St Nicholas' Church were said to have been sent to London - to be made into stones for grinding down grain into flour. And at nearby Gorleston, a vicar was supposed to have cleared gravestones out of the churchyard of St Andrew's around 1800 - and sold them to a baker for lining his ovens.

The story goes that for years afterwards you would get down to the bottom of your loaf to discover 'aged 75 years' pressed in it....!

Rotten Rivals and Deadly Duels

And while we're on the subject of death (which, let's face it, we seem to be on rather a lot!), let's look at what happened when people decided to take a violent dislike to each other.

Sometimes fatal, always nasty.

The Battling Brothers
One of the nastiest Norfolk stories concerns the fight between Sir William Gerbygge and his brother over some land.

They started argu-ing and then things got very violent - so violent, in fact, that in their fury they tore out each other's hearts. And God was so upset by this (although I can't imagine either of the

brothers was exactly overjoyed either) that he turned them both to stone. In Wickhampton church there's an stone effigy (sculpture) of Sir W holding a heart...

A nice nasty bit of folklore. But history has taken its own nasty turns - let's go see...

Deadly Duels
Sooner or later when you watch a soap on telly there'll be a situation like this: Person A takes a dislike to Person B. They meet in the street and there's a lot of pushing, snarling and finger-pointing...

...then someone pulls each of them back by the shoulders and says 'Leave him/her alone, he/she's not worth it...'

But back in olden times things were very different.

If someone insulted (or was said to have insulted) another person, then a challenge to a duel was issued. That meant that at a certain time (usually in some isolated spot), the two people in the argument would turn up with a 'second' (their helper) and fight it out to see who was right.

One of the most famous duels happened in 1599 between Sir Robert Mansfield (or Mansell) and Sir John Heydon.

They fought about a kilometre from Barford Bridge. Sir John was injured in several places 'but the deadly wound was by a thrust in at his throat and out of the top of his head'.

Sir Robert left the injured Sir John and went away, expecting to hear about his death within a few hours. But Sir John didn't - he recovered.

Well, all except his chopped-off hand, that is. And, amazingly, you can still see the hand in Norwich Castle where it has to be one of their best gory exhibits.

You'd have thought that having such an injury would have knocked some sense into Sir John. But it didn't.

He tried to fight the Earl of Essex in 1614 even though he only had one hand. The earl had to be held back by the Archbishop of Canterbury ('Leave him alone, Essex, he's not wurff it') and the Queen was so upset at the fight in her palace that she chucked Sir John into prison to teach him a lesson.

Still, you've got to hand it to Sir John.

Er, or maybe not.

In 1699 Sir Sewster Peyton fought a duel with a Mr King at Attleborough (and, no, we don't know whether he'd caught Mr K laughing at his name). It was bad news for King - he was killed.

But as the years went by it became frowned upon to settle fights in this way - although there was no shortage of angry young men prepared to fight duels if they could. Thomas Roope of Lakenham was fined 40 shillings (£2) and put in jail in 1811 for issuing a challenge to Robert Alderson of Norwich the August before.

The court decided that Roope had intended 'great bodily harm and mischief'.

And there was another great row when Lempster Bulkeney of the 40th Regiment got into a dispute with William Simpson in Norwich on June 21 1826.

There was an 'altercation' and a scuffle. Bulkeney then went round telling every-one that he had given Simpson 'a damned good thrashing'.

Simpson was furious at this version of events and said Bulkeney was lying. So the army man challenged Simpson to a duel.

And that's when the brave soldier suddenly decided to chicken out. There was a series of bad-tempered letters between the two, then our friend Bulkeney backed out of the duel completely.

Simpson, furious, later wrote: 'I have since publicly insulted Mr Bulkeney by striking him and calling him a coward to his face.'

He also wrote to Bulkeney's regiment to tell them what a wuss he was. Did Bulkeney finally come out and fight? Nope - he ran to the local magistrates. And they ordered Simpson to stop stirring things.

So he printed a leaflet all about the duel-that-never-was and spread it all over the city.

Now, now boys. Behave!

Mouldering Murderers, Part 1

Norfolk has had its fair share of cruel killers - and some just ended up here, thinking they could escape justice. Let's meet the most famous one of those... and some other vile villains.

Awful Aram

Eugene Aram was a brilliant scholar and teacher, who worked in King's Lynn in the 1750s. He should have been most famous for his discoveries about the roots of Europe's languages.

But it was his guilty secret which has made his name live on... even if he didn't.

In 1744, while in his home county of Yorkshire, he murdered his friend Daniel Clark. For 14 years he escaped justice - but while he was at Lynn, the authorities caught up with him, and Aram was executed in 1759.

The Victorians loved his story, because it had a moral message they were always

'Please, sir, how do you spell "murderer"?'

trying to teach their children: your sins will find you out.

It inspired a novel and - more famously - a poem by Thomas Hood, which ends with the lines...

'Two stern-faced men set out from Lynn,
Through the cold and heavy mist;
And Eugene Aram walk'd between,
With gyves [shackles] upon his wrist.'

Wretched Robbers

Robbery has always been a strong motive for murder. In 1635 Thomas Heath was robbed and murdered near Sheringham, and a monument to the unlucky man was set up in the parish church.

Exactly one hundred years later a group of Dutch sailors was drinking in the Bird in Hand pub in Row 108 in Great Yarmouth. One was left behind while his fellow countrymen moved on to other places.

The man's brother came back to the pub a few hours later to pick him up - only to find the pub shut up and a pistol being fired at him. That was a bad sign.

'Now "ear's" something truly nasty!'

But even worse was a bit later when the body of the Dutchman turned up in the river... *without his ears*. They had had gold rings in them, which made them attractive to desperate robbers.

Elizabeth Thompson, the landlady of the pub, her daughter and eight others were arrested. Only Thompson ended up on trial, and she made the fateful (and fatal) decision not to reveal who the real murderers had been. She was hanged.

Robbers were the root of another murder story, this time at Gorleston. A hill at the edge of the cliff was known in the early 19th century as 'Deadman's Hill'.

Here's why. One day. a traveller wanted to be taken from a ship to the shore.

He got into a boat with his large - and heavy - chest.

The boatmen waited until the ship was out of sight, then turned on the traveller and murdered him.

They all later built homes on the hill, but none had much luck in life after their terrible crime. None of the townsfolk could prove anything, but all they had their suspicions about why the boatmen had suddenly got rich.

One of the boatmen was later found guilty of robbery and sent to a convicts' colony in Australia - where in 1826 he finally confessed, on his deathbed, to his earlier crime.

'I said "I'm an evil killer", not "I need a koala"!'

Capital crimes

Two Norfolk killers committed their terrible crimes outside the county - and found a place in history.

James Greenacre, who was born in 1785 at North Runcton, was executed in May 1837 for the killing in London of Hannah Brown, who was also born in Norfolk.

But Greenacre had nearly ended up in big trouble in 1820 when he was part of the Cato Street Conspiracy - a dastardly plot to murder leading Government ministers and start a revolution. Five of the conspirators were executed for their part in the plan.

John Tawell - known as 'Tawell the Quaker' - was even more notorious. He came from Burgh St Peter or Aldeby, and was sent as a convict in Australia for forging a £10 note in London, before being pardoned in 1820 and returning back to England.

He became quite wealthy by opening a chemist shop and eventually returned to London. He married, but when his wife became ill he started an affair with her nurse.

His wife died in 1838, and Tawell married a Mrs Cutforth in 1841. But he still went on seeing his lover, Sarah Hart, and moved her to a place called Salt Hill, near Slough.

But then Tawell decided to kill his lover by poisoning her, either in her beer or in an apple.

When he tried to escape by rail, the police used the newly-invented electric telegraph to alert their colleagues in London - who were waiting to nab Tawell when he got off the train.

It was the first time in history that the telegraph had helped catch a criminal.

The Guilty Wife
We started with a story of guilty secrets catching up with a killer in Lynn - and we'll end with one too.

And it's an even more fascinating one.

Two books, one from 1599 and one from 1612, tell how sometime in the 1590s a travelling company of actors - the Earl of Sussex's Men - were performing a play called 'The History of Friar Francis' in St George's Guildhall (now Lynn Arts Centre).

The play was about the story of a wife who murdered her husband and was then haunted by his ghost.

At one performance a woman in the audience screamed out when the 'ghost' came on stage: 'Oh my husband! My husband! I see the ghost of my husband fiercely threatening and menacing me!'

When she had stopped screaming she confessed that seven years earlier she had poisoned her husband so she could be with her lover.

A writer was so struck by the amazing story that he decided to use it in one of his own plays. The lines he wrote were...

'I have heard/ That guilty creatures sitting at a play/ Have by the very cunning of the scene/Been struck to the soul, that presently/They have proclaimed their malefactions [bad actions].'

The play? Hamlet (Act II Scene 2).

The playwright? You've already guessed, haven't you... William Shakespeare.

And it isn't the only time the words 'ghost' and 'murder' are in the same Norfolk story. But for more, we'll have to go to another chapter...

Mouldering Murderers, Part 2

The Haunted Husband
William Sheward of Norwich
was fed up with his wife
moaning at him all the time.
Until one day in 1851, in a fit
of temper, he killed her.

He got rid of her body
(don't ask) and managed to
cover up his crime for 18
years - but he was said to
have been haunted by her
ghost at the foot of his bed
until he could stand it no
longer. In 1869 he confessed to his crime - and was hanged
at Norwich Castle.

The Ghastly Gibbet
We've met gibbets before, but for those who've forgotten
it was the custom for really, really bad villains to have their
hanged remains covered in tar (to preserve them) and then
hung up in a metal cage near the scenes of their crimes.

The Rev Augustus Jessopp (yes, the same chap who saw
the mysterious visitor at Mannington Hall) told of a man
called Downes who had been crossing Bradenham Heath in a
storm.

Downes had meant to keep a couple of kilometres between
himself and the swinging, creaking remains of the dead criminal, but somehow he ended up being close.

Too close.

He rode his horse closer and closer to the gibbet until it was directly above his head.

Then there was a loud scream (and no, it wasn't him). His horse was terrified, swerved, banging Downes' leg against the gibbet and something fell down.

Downes looked down and saw... the murderer's leg bone.

The Haunted Horse
We've met spooky horses already - but this story from Thetford is a horse with a difference.

In 1569 young Lord Dacre was murdered by his sinister guardian Sir Richard Fulmerston. Cunning Sir Richard had messed about with Dacre's rocking horse so that the little lord would fall off, and die from the impact.

He did - but little Dacre had the last word. His ghost is said to prance up and down on a headless rocking horse at the Nunnery.

And talking of Thetford, there's supposed to be a secret room in King's House in which the skeleton of a murdered man sits at a table with a parchment in front of him, with all the doors and windows nailed up...

The Spooky Saxon
We have to go back to before the Norman Conquest for the next scary story.

It happened in the ninth century. The woodman Bern murdered Danish king Ragnar and ran away to Denmark - telling everyone that the East Anglian king Edmund had done the evil deed.

The furious Danes invaded - and fought and killed King
Edmund. As for Bern, his ghost is still said to race through
Reedham once a year, pursued by Saxon archers determined
to avenge their betrayed king...

Sands of time
The dunes at Great Yarmouth have seen several murders
over the years. One place where a murder was committed in
early Victorian times is supposed to be haunted by a tall man
with an evil expression, who walks up and down talking to
himself. It's the murderer, returning to the scene of the
crime...

Dead Strange

Of course, being murdered isn't the only way people have met their end. But sometimes their exits have been, well, just plain weird...

...Lighting your pipe

Mr Lym, a tailor from King's Lynn, was settling down to enjoy his pipe in January 1812 when something unexpected happened.

It exploded.

Someone, the little scamp, had decided it would be a really, *really* funny practical joke to put gunpowder in his tobacco.

But Mr Lym wasn't around to share the joke - or catch the culprit. You see the joker had put too much explosive in the tobacco, and the tailor was killed instantly.

Well, anyone could have told him that smoking is bad for your health...

...Taking out your tooth

Take a tip from us. If you have toothache, go to the dentist to sort it out. Don't try to do what a Norfolk farmworker did, as reported at an inquest in January 1930.

He had a bad tooth but decided he would save money by taking it out himself. Only trouble is, he used the same dirty horrible penknife he used to cut up his lunch with.

He died of tetanus.

...Tempting fate

On December 27 1860 a clown, Thomas Algar, was performing in the Great Yarmouth panto. He had just said the lines '...got touched upon the sleeve familiarly, by Death himself...' - when he fell down dead.

'He' really was behind you that time. Oh yes he was!

...Becoming a mayor

Being elected the mayor of your town is a great honour. But not in Lynn in 1558, according to one tradition, anyway.

Mayor Number One was elected.

And died of the plague.

Along came Mayor Number Two. Er, until he died of the plague.

As did Mayor Number Three. And Four. And Five...

...Ringing a bell

In 1806 James Coleman was ringing the bell at Swardeston parish church when something rather unexpected happened. It fell through two floors and ended up on his head.

In 1621 there was another bell-related accident. This time it was an unlucky ringer at St Margaret's Church in Lynn.

He was pulling the Great Bell when he forgot to let go of the rope. Oops.

We could have 'tolled' him that was a silly thing to do...

...Having your fortune told

If you're a fortune teller what your customers really want to hear is something about winning the Lottery or some other nice surprise. But the fortune teller who was talking to a Mrs Holland of Great Yarmouth in 1815 was obviously a bit fed up with doing that.

So, for fun, she decided to tell her some really scary stories instead.

A bit too scary. You see, Mrs Holland was frightened to death... literally.

'You will meet a tall dark stranger, with evil sticky-out eyes and big teeth and...'

...Patting your dog

Dr Saunders was out shooting partridges near Gunton Old Hall in September 1814 when he stooped down to pat his dog for bringing back a bird he'd shot. Only he'd forgotten that his gun was still loaded...

...and pointing at himself.

Not nice.

...Playing football

The early version of footy, 'camping', was a vicious affair in which the players got kicked more than the ball. In the Martham church registers for 1619, there's one entry under the 'deaths' bit for John Smyth, who 'broke his leg at the football'...

...Being a hero

In 1812 a quick-thinking man on Yarmouth pier spotted a boat in trouble so threw out a thick rope from the quayside to the boatmen.

One slight problem. He'd forgotten to get out of the way first.

He was dragged over the side, to his doom.

...Overdoing the pickled herring

Elizabethan writer Robert Greene didn't believe in doing anything by halves. Even dying.

Born in 1558 in Norwich, the playwright and writer (if he seems familiar, that's because we've met him in 'NASTY NORWICH', moaning about Shakespeare pinching his idea for a play) wrote about living a good and pure life.

Only trouble was, he spent all his money (and his poor wife's) on booze and riotous living. When his wife moved out in disgust, taking their son with her, you'd have thought Greene would have mended his ways. Not a bit of it - he moved from Norwich to London and became even more wild.

Then in August 1592 he met his Maker after over-indulging in wine...and pickled herring.

As he lay dying he wrote a letter to his wife begging her forgiveness.

Oh, and if she could just pay the letter-carrier the £10 Greene owed him...

...Dissolving your local monastery
After Henry VIII ordered all the monasteries to close, it was the signal for lots of greedy landowners to get their hands on the land.

Most of the buildings were pulled down within a few years so the materials could be sold off. Only sometimes things didn't go quite go to plan...

Edward Paston was pulling down Binham Priory when a workman was killed by falling masonry - so he gave up.

Then there's Sir Roger Townshend, who began to knock down the church at Coxford Abbey. The first stone which fell off broke a man's leg. And when the steeple was pulled over it plunged straight into the house of a very surprised peasant called Mr Seller, who had broken his leg playing football (now, where have we heard that before?).

Sir Roger knew when the fates were against him. He gave up.

...Not ducking
In 1836 the Rev Richard Pillans of Larling was heading into the Angel Inn at the corner of Yarmouth market place when he made two mistakes.

Mistake number one: he hadn't lowered his carriage seat.

Mistake number two: he didn't notice the Angel Inn's beam coming to meet him.

Ouch.

Mouldy Mariners and Silly Sailors

So far most of our stories have been on dry land. But, of course, Norfolk is a coastal county and so for the next couple of chapters we'll take a look at some of its sea-flavoured tales - historical and spooky.

Bearly alive...

Let's say hello to our first mariner, Captain Cook from King's Lynn. He had a whaler - a ship which went out to capture the poor long-suffering whales in the stormy northern seas. He returned home in August 1788 from a voyage to Greenland with an even hairier adventure to talk about than usual.

On the way he'd met gales and icebergs. But that wasn't the worst bit. When he arrived on shore in Greenland he was grabbed by a polar bear.

As the bear hugged him close, the captain screamed out to the ship's surgeon to SHOOT THE BEAR!!!! (He may have used a naughty word in there too). Luckily for Cap'n Cook (but unluckily for the bear), the surgeon was a brilliant shot and managed to kill the bear even though it was more than 40 metres away.

The Unlucky Admiral

Poor Sir Cloudesley Shovell had managed to live through a lot of misfortune since being born at Cockthorpe in North Norfolk in 1650. Well, being called 'Cloudesley Shovell' mostly.

But the sailor had steadily risen through the ranks to become a brave and successful admiral.

He survived an abscess (swelling) on his throat in 1695, and survived again in 1703 when the Great Storm struck while he was at sea (he survived, 100 ships off Great Yarmouth didn't).

He must have thought he had a guardian angel. Well, maybe he did, but in October 1707 the angel was obviously on holiday.

For poor Sir C was left crashing into the deadly rocks off the Isles of Scilly, near Cornwall, after an error in navigation. More than 1800 sailors were swept to their deaths in the tragedy.

And there's a tradition that Sir Cloudesley was washed up alive, only to be murdered by islanders for his rings.

The perilous passage

For centuries, ships tried to find a way to get to the rich lands of China, India and what is now Indonesia. They could sail round the bottom of Africa or South America, but many tried to find a way through the iceberg-filled waters north of Canada instead.

This search for the 'North West Passage' was to cost many lives.

When the Victorian explorer Sir John Franklin disappeared on one of these expeditions, Lynn mariner Lieutenant Sam Cresswell was one of those sent on HMS Investigator to try and find him.

The rescuers soon needed rescuing themselves. The ship spent two terrible winters stuck in the Arctic, constantly in danger from the icebergs and with the crew having to eat rotting meat in tins and drinking water which had been spoiled by salt.

Lt Cresswell set off on the ice with some of his sailors, dragging sledges behind them and desperately trying to live off the frozen meat which was all they had left. Amazingly, the weak, desperate band was picked up by another ship and Cresswell was sent back to Lynn, where he arrived in late October 1853.

His family were overjoyed to see him - they had long since given him up for dead.

And Lt Cresswell was greeted as a hero, because he was the first person to tell England about the discovery of the fabled ocean route.

But this was a story without a happy ending. Poor Samuel was so devastated by his ordeal that he died aged just 39.

98

Fryer of the Bounty

And talking about ordeals, that endured by John Fryer - who was born at Wells in 1752 - is one of the most famous in naval history. He was master of the exploration ship HMS Bounty when the crew rebelled ('mutinied') against its captain, a man called Bligh.

Bligh, Fryer and a few others were set adrift in a small boat in the Pacific Ocean. But if the mutineers thought they had sealed their fate, they were wrong. Fryer and co managed to sail thousands of miles without any sort of maps to reach safety.

'NOW will you admit they weren't joking?'

It was an epic journey of incredible determination. But the trip had left its toll on the Norfolk man, who never really recovered from his ordeal. He died back home in Wells in May 1817. But the story of the 'Mutiny on the Bounty' lives on in films and books.

Window Paine

Not quite so worthy of praise was the pirate William Paine, whose villainous exploits we've met in 'NASTY NORFOLK'. Paine was eventually hanged in London for his crimes but his remains were supposed to be sent back to Great Yarmouth for gibbeting.

Trouble is, none of the coach firms wanted to carry a dead pirate, thank you very much. So the story goes that Paine's body was put in a box with the words 'GLASS - WITH CARE' on it. And it arrived, safe and sound, in Yarmouth. Just as well no one opened it up on the journey. That really *would* have been a shattering experience...

Spooky Sea and Creepy Coast

The words 'sea' and 'strange tales' were just made for each other. And here's the proof…

The curse of the yow-yows

There's a spot just opposite a cliff at Sheringham which has a very spooky reputation. It's here, according to a 19th-century legend, that a captain was once drowned. Ever since then, fishermen have every now and then heard a sound like a human voice coming from the water.

But if they pull towards the noise it pops up in another direction. Then, finally, it sounds like it is coming from beneath the boat - and that's the signal for the men to row hard for the shore.

'No, it's "yow-yows", not "Ow-ows"!'

Because the 'yow-yow' - as the noise is known - is followed by a brief and violent gust of wind (squall), which can tip a boat over.

The vanishing man

One day during the second world war a man was fishing off the Wellington Pier at Great Yarmouth. A stranger came up and started chatting to him - but then a German plane suddenly appeared, flying low and machine-gunning everything in sight.

The angler threw himself down until the plane had flown by a couple of seconds later. He got up - and he was absolutely alone. He asked the people at the gate to the pier - the only way in or out to the pier - and they had seen no one else...

Smugglers' tales

The Norfolk coast has always been a tempting place for smugglers to bring ashore illicit cargoes - whether it be brandy from France or anything else the authorities had either banned or stuck a big tax on.

With the profits so huge, there have been cases of smugglers who turned to even darker deeds to keep their secrets.

Like the famous spook known as the 'Haisbro' Pump Hill Ghost'. Around the year 1800 several Happisburgh farmers reported seeing a ghost dragging a mysterious heavy bundle to a well.

When someone looked into the well they found a man's body with the head still on (just) but the legs chopped off and

'Er... he's definitely not well...'

in a separate bag. It's thought that the man was a smuggler who had been murdered by his fellow crooks, and chopped up to make it easier to get rid of his body.

We bet it was a long, long time before anyone could face a drink from that particular well...

More dirty deeds over at Somerton, where the ghost of a girl walks the shore with her head under her arm and crying over and over again.

It's said she was murdered by a gang of smugglers and buried alongside the cliff.

But one day her cliff grave was disturbed - and so she will haunt the coast until her bones are re-discovered and buried properly in a churchyard....

The Long Coastguardsman
Another famous Norfolk ghost is this chap, who is found from Bacton to Mundesley on the darkest nights - around midnight, naturally.

Sometimes he shouts for help, sometimes he laughs - and sometimes (like during a gale) he sings and shouts.

The Victorian writer Ernest Suffling told the story and said 'I nearly met him once between midnight and one o'clock at a place called Ostend, near Walcott'.

'I can "sea" you're scary...'

Suffling noticed a shadow flitting along, keeping to the darkest parts of the beach...

But the 'spook' turned out to be another sort of night visitor: a poacher!

Cromer creepy bits
Several hundred years ago there was a village to the north of where Cromer is now, called Shipden.

And it's said that the old village church bells still ring on Christmas Day... and also when there's about to be a shipwreck.

Another Cromer tale was told about the church. A man was crossing the path through the graveyard one night early in the 19th century when he saw a little child-like figure, dressed in white, rising from the ground.

The figure steadily grew in height until its face was level with the terrified man - and then 'a sudden gash appeared across its throat, blood rushing onto clothes, then vanished like a flash'.

Theatre tales

The old Windmill Theatre on Yarmouth seafront was built in the early years of the last century. Staff have regularly reported hauntings over the years, and Jack Jay - who bought the theatre in 1937 - used to tell how he had heard ghostly actors reciting lines.

When the building was taken over in the early 1990s, the new staff were puzzled by doors flying open for no reason, people who suddenly appeared then vanished, feelings that 'someone was watching' and even taped announcements switching on by themselves at midnight.

The Shrieking Pits of Aylmerton

One of the most famous Norfolk ghost stories - right up there with the Brown Lady of Raynham Hall and Sir Thomas Boleyn - is this celebrated tale, which dates back to at least the middle of the 19th century.

A Victorian amateur archaeologist wrote in 1850 how a village worker had told him cries were frequently heard from the pits and that a woman dressed in white 'rose ever and anon screaming from among them, and ran from one to another, looking down into them, wringing her hands and shrieking'.

The labourer even told the writer that the woman in white had once followed him home!

Not so well known is the tale told about Runton Mill, a little further along the coast. There a ghostly light is seen crossing a nearby field and burying itself in a little cluster of trees... where human bones were once found.

Mysterious monsters

It's huge, the sea. But big enough to have unknown monsters in it?

In August 1936, the readers of the Eastern Evening News were told of a series of sightings of a 'sea serpent' off the coast at Eccles. Former city Lord Mayor Mr H E Witard spotted something about nine metres long travelling at around 60 miles per hour.

'I am positive that what we saw was a sea serpent,' he said.

'Well, I can't see anything – are you SURE you saw a sea serpent?'

'We were all on the beach together in the evening when we saw the creature, and it was a perfectly clear evening.

'The creature looked like a huge snake. Its action in the swimming was worm-like, and not the roll of a porpoise.'

He said the creature had been about a mile off and heading towards Happisburgh.

Letters flooded in from people who said Mr Witard must have mistaken a fast-flying flock of ducks for a creature - a Mr J J Hall said a similar thing had fooled him off Gorleston in 1930.

But then other people wrote in saying that they had seen a creature at least 13 metres long swimming off Beeston, Cromer and Overstrand a couple of days after Mr Witard's sighting.

And one reader wrote in to say that in 1935 he had seen a mysterious sea animal washed up on Eccles beach. 'It had a fish-like body, the bones of an animal and small feathers in the neck and also a long thick tail similar to a crocodile,' he said. The creature had been buried on the beach.

Perhaps it's still there...

Nasty Nature

From tales of mythical creatures to real ones....

Norfolk has always had plenty of animals and birds (and other creatures).

But it's also had lots of people. And when people and creatures meet - well, guess who usually ends up on the losing side?

Let's meet the nastier face of nature...

Wretched wrens
Who could be horrible to this tiny and very sweet little bird, only 9.5cm long and weighing just nine grams? Humans, that's who. It used to be a countryside tradition to hunt them every St Stephen's Day (Boxing Day) because Norfolk folk thought that on that particular day witches would change into the shape of a wren.

Kill a wren, kill a witch. Simple - and stupid.

And at the other end of the scale...

Whopping whales
As well as the boats which used to go out to catch whales (like the Lynn whalers we mentioned a couple of chapters ago), the huge mammals sometimes washed up on the shore by themselves (and still do).

For centuries it's been the right of kings and queens to be offered automatically any whales which turn up on our shores. In 1857 a whale came ashore at Winterton - so Queen Victoria was asked if she wanted it. She didn't.

Perhaps she got wind of what was to happen at Happisburgh a bit later on in her reign. A massive whale, more than 20 metres long, washed up on the village beach.

'Goody,' said the villagers, 'This'll bring in lots of tourists!'

Which it did. Who promptly ate and drank everything in Happisburgh. The villagers had to go hungry until more food supplies arrived.

And then an even bigger problem happened. Natural decay had got to work on our mega-mammal with the inevitable result that it began to pong.

And how! It reeked - you could smell it almost two kilometres away.

See what we mean about Queen Victoria getting wind of it?

Monstrous maggots
Talking about decay is a good moment to bring in a bit of wildlife you might not want popping up on your plate.
Maggots. Wriggly, yucky, gooey maggots.

But some Norfolk people did.

Yes, really.

William Marshall, the farm agent on the Gunton estate, wrote in 1780 that Norfolk farmers were to blame for 'allowing their cheeses to be devoured, year after year, by maggots'.

But what was worse was that some people got so used to it that they actually *preferred* cheese with the maggots wriggling away. A bit of extra meat, we suppose.

Tuck into your breakfast, there. What's that? You've lost your appetite?

Ruff justice

The poor wren isn't the only bird to end up on the receiving end in Norfolk. Not by a long chirp.

We've heard in 'NASTY NORFOLK' how the great crested grebe was hunted so its feathers could be used in ladies' fashions. The poor old ruff also made the mistake of being very distinctive, with a frill of feathers round its head or neck.

Thousands were netted: some were killed straight away and others fattened up for market.

So many were killed that it largely vanished in the county from 1898 until 1963.

Other species didn't fare much  better. So often the cry went up: 'Oooh, what a rare and interesting bird – I know, let's shoot it!'

Two eagles were shot near Great Yarmouth in 1803 - one had a magnificent 2.4m wingspan. Which made it an even easier target.

In 1818 a man killed nine of 'that rare bird called the golden plover' with one shot.

Sorry, that should have now read 'that even *rarer* bird...'

And so it went on.

In 1830 the first recorded sightings of the red-footed falcon were made at Horning. It was shot.

In the following year, England's last great bustard - a huge turkey-like bird a metre long - was killed near Thetford.

And the story of the poor old Bohemian waxwing sums it all up.

The rare bird was spotted at Old Buckenham in November 1866. One was seen the same day at Thetford and - BANG! - it was shot. By the first week in December, 22 had been spotted and killed.

By the end of that month, 100 had been blasted out of the sky and sent to the taxidermists to be stuffed.

Happy new year?

Not for the poor Bohemian waxwing.

William Dutt, in his 1900 book on Norfolk, talked about: 'the unfortunate lot of strange birds seeking to establish themselves in England. They have always been ruthlessly murdered.'

Gory Geese

Mind you, it wasn't just wild birds which ended up on the receiving end. In November 1897 the Norfolk and Norwich Society for the Prevention of Cruelty to Animals took two people from Terrington St Clement to court for being cruel to 130 geese by plucking them - *while they were still alive.*

'The practice, it was said, was not uncommon a quarter of a century previously but it had since ceased except in remote localities,' said the report.

The court heard the practice was 'unquestionably barbarous and cruel'.

A witness for the defendants told the court that as a 'goose puller' he had plucked 1500 live birds every year. If birds had their feathers pulled out, he explained, it was supposed to increase their weight.

Guess what? The men got off.

'Orrible Otters
Who could wallop an otter? But for centuries the cute whiskered river creatures were hunted and bashed for their fur, because they ate fish - or just for the fun of it. Otter hunts (with special otter hounds) used to go through the Broads in search of the unlucky creature.

One writer told (in the early 1890s) how 'a few' were still caught '...and a most delightful and exciting sport it must have been'.

Er, put your hand up anyone who disagrees with that. Thought so. Too many hands to count.

Sad Squirrels
Equally cute is the squirrel, especially the (now very rare) red variety. The Rev Richard Forby, writing at the end of the 18th century, said it was the Norfolk custom to hunt squirrels on Christmas Day - with men and boys chasing the poor creatures from tree to tree with sticks and stones.

Have a Merry Christmas, Mr Nutkin.

Rotten Rabbits
Bunnies have always had a special place in the life of Norfolk, as their meat was a common part of the diet for many ordinary country folk, and their fur (especially the silver-

grey variety once common around Thetford and Winterton) was used to make clothes.

But balanced with the helpful hand the rabbits gave to local farmers was their destructive nature - they will munch their way through crops and breed, well, like rabbits.

Thousands were shot or netted in the area around Brandon and Thetford, but by the 1940s numbers were beginning to fall because of the use of poison gas.

There was an even more horrible way of controlling them, a virus called myxomatosis which left the rabbits blind and with a terrible fever.

To give some idea of how big the impact was, on Scolt Head Island (near Brancaster) there were perhaps 10,000 rabbits in 1954. By January 1955, there were just 12.

Over the years the rabbits have developed ways of resisting the virus, but there are still outbreaks from time to time. But wild bunnies are here to stay - despite the nasty virus (and being bashed by passing cars).

Bishop Beaver
You'd have thought that the last thing the wildlife of the county would want to do was actually go out of its way to help humans.

But according to one Norfolk legend, that's just what happened around AD600 when St Felix sailed up the river to Babingley in West Norfolk to bring Christianity to East Anglia.

His boat was shipwrecked - but he was saved by passing beavers, who helped him build his first church.

And in gratitude he made one of the beavers a bishop!

In case you're wondering 'Hang on a minute, beavers?', there really were beavers in this country until possibly as late as the 15th century. So what happened to them?

Well, if we said their fur was sought-after, we think you can guess the rest...

Beer – and Spirits

For our next look at Norfolk's rich legacy of spooky stories we take a look at those specially associated with pubs and hotels.

And there are lots of them, which may have something to do with the fact that many of the buildings date back hundreds of years... or that drink enough booze and you'll end up seeing things. Usually the ceiling while flat out on the floor!

It's a ghost, deer
And one of those spectral sights was noted by Harriet Martineau, a famous 19th-century Norwich writer. She used to tell a story of how when she was a little girl she was terrified of the spectral stag said to come out of a pub near St Augustine's Gate...

'It's either a ghost – or it's a stag night'

The wicked servant
The Queen's Head pub was in the High Street at King's Lynn until it was demolished and the land used to build a shop instead. But while it was a pub it was haunted by the ghost of a maidservant and her boyfriend who were executed in 1731 for murdering the servant's boss.

Kett's victim

The Adam and Eve pub near Norwich Cathedral is said to
have a very posh spook - the ghost of Tudor big cheese Lord
Sheffield. The toff lost his life nearby during the bloody
1549 Kett's Rebellion.

Ferry, ferry scary

The Old Ferry Inn at Horning is thought to have been a
storehouse for mead (a type of booze) for the monks of St
Benet's Abbey.

And too much drink and some wicked monks is the back-
ground for the story of the Grey Lady (Green Lady in some
versions) who is said to haunt the pub.

The story goes that while the monks were drunk they
attacked and murdered her, then chucked her body into the
river to try and hide their crime.

The pub's owner, Mr A R Stringer, told in August 1954
how, before the war (and the pub was badly bombed in 1941)
he had seen a 'trail of vapour' drifting through the bar after
a door banged.

After the war he had heard chanting and singing in the
pub's loft, and one of his workers had seen the Grey Lady
going through the rooms before vanishing into the river...

The Creepy Coachmaker

The landlord of the Coachmakers' Arms in St Stephen's,
Norwich, was startled by the unexpected visitor who turned
up in December 1975 - a man dressed in 18th-century
costume, complete with a three-cornered hat.

His presence was blamed for the mysterious turning
upside down of a coffee table, and for the taps of the gas
used to pump the beer turning on and off by themselves.

Betty's back

One of Thetford's most celebrated haunted places is the

Bell Inn, which is said to be the home of the ghost of one of its former landladies, Betty Radcliffe.

She was murdered on the site by her lover, the inn's stableman....

Inn trouble...
Our last story was first written down in 1736, but spoke of events happening 'many years ago' at an inn at Magdalen Street in Norwich.

A visitor to the pub was struck by the portrait hanging there of a very pale-looking man dressed in a black outfit of a bygone age. He asked at the pub who the person was, but no-one seemed to know.

Then one night when he was walking near the Cathedral gates he saw a man with a swollen face, a rope round his neck and a knife in his chest - an executioner's knife. The man realised with terror that it was the same man as in the picture. The apparition gave a deep groan - then vanished.

The man eventually found an old Roman Catholic priest who told him it was the picture of the Rev Thomas Tunstal, executed in 1616 at the Magdalen Street gates.

Bloody Battles

Norfolk has been fought over by several armies over the centuries. Some conflicts are well known (like the Siege of King's Lynn and our old friend Kett's Rebellion), but other fights now belong in the realms of folklore.

Often they were people's way of explaining mysterious earthworks which dot the Norfolk countryside. So, for instance, the 12 burial mounds near Great Snarehill, near Thetford, were explained by some as being where the last King of East Anglia, Edmund, was defeated and captured by the Danes.

Bronze Age burial barrows at Bergh Apton also inspired a tradition, recorded in 1850, that a battle had been fought on White Heath.

There's one thing that many of these traditions share: that the battles fought there were not wussy ones but instead were full-scale, chop-their-heads-off and die-in-horrible-ways ones.

Land near West Bilney church was known as Bloodfields, after a gory Civil War fight said to have taken place there.

And Blood Hills near West Somerton is said to have got its name from a battle between the Saxons and the Danes where so much blood was shed that the slopes ran red. And a similar story is told of the fort (which was actually built in the Iron Age) at Bloodgate Hill, near South Creake.

The Saxons and Danes were also supposed to have clashed at a field called Blood's Dale at Drayton.

Jack O'Lanterns and Fairy Folk

We've met plenty of strange creatures in our look at Norfolk's folklore so far. Lots of ghosts, of course, but also mysterious sea creatures, the Devil, Black Shuck and Spring-Heeled Jack.

Let's meet a couple more, shall we?

Scary Jack

This mysterious chap was a fearful inhabitant of the Broads. Jack - also known as Hob-o'-Lantern or the Lantern Man - would lure unwary travellers to their doom in the marshes by flashing a light on dark nights.

The traveller would think that someone was trying to guide him to safety, so would step towards the light - only to plunge into the boggy, treacherous marshes where there was no-one to hear his desperate pleas for help.

The sightings were similar to that of a spectral herdsman who would drive helpless cattle into a swampy 'pulk hole' where they got stuck.

Emily Cranworth, writing around 1900, quoted an old servant of hers who had seen the lantern man 'scores of times'.

Here's what he told her (and it's in Norfolk dialect spelling): 'Folks du say that if one man stand at one end of the field, and another man stand over agin him in the other corner, and they will whistle each to other, the lantern man will always run to the whistle.

'It is good thing to know this, as the lantern man will always try to come agin you and to kill ye, if so be he is able...'

The legend of Heard's Holde

One of the most celebrated Jack O'Lantern sightings was recalled by the remarkable Anna Lubbock, known as the 'Washerwoman of Irstead', whose huge range of local sayings, superstitions and stories was fortunately recorded by a far-sighted clergyman, the Rev John Gunn, in the 1840s.

As Anna was born in 1766, her stories are an important link to the beliefs of the ordinary people of Norfolk right back into the 18th century. Her stories about Heard's Holde - in the Alder Carr Fen Broad near Neatishead, all dated from before 1810.

Jack O'Lantern was often seen in the spot on a 'roky' [misty] night. 'I have often seen it there,' Anna told the vicar, 'rising up and falling, and twistering about, and then up again. It looked exactly like a candle in a lantern.'

Mrs Lubbock said the spirit was that of a man called Heard (also given as Hearne in some stories), 'guilty of some unmentionable crimes', who drowned there. Travellers who walked along with a lantern near the spot risked enraging Jack if he appeared and they did not immediately put out their lights.

'Jack would come against it and dash it to pieces; and that a gentlemen who made a mock of him, was riding on horseback one evening in Horning, when he came at him and knocked him off his horse.'

Eventually the Neatishead people got so fed up with Jack's antics that three of them set out to lay his spirit - by using the Bible's words to stop him haunting. But as they read the verses, Jack kept one step ahead by reading the next verse before them. Then a village

'Coo, this'll get Jack in a flap!'

boy brought a couple of pigeons, which so distracted Jack that his spirit was bound after all.

Jack and Giles
This story (dating to at least 1900) is told about Cromer, which shows that Jack sometimes stepped outside the Broads - if he was sure of giving someone a good scare, that is!

A young man was walking along one night when he saw the lantern man coming for him - so ran desperately for the safety of a cottage where old Giles lived.

'O Giles, for heaven's sake, let me in - the lantern man's coming!' he screamed.

Giles told him not to be such a fool as there was no such thing - but looked up and saw the apparition for himself, so hurried to open the door.

Giles tried attaching a lit candle in a lamp on the end of a pole to try to draw Jack off - but the lantern man just 'burst it all to pieces'.

The story ends with this piece of advice: 'They do say, if the lantern man light upon you, the best thing is to throw yourself flat on your face and hold your breath.'

So where do all these lantern men stories come from? This is one case where we can point to a scientific explanation, as sometimes rotting vegetation will give off a gas which ignites by itself - easy to mistake as a lamp carried by a fellow traveller on a dark and stormy night....

But there's one story which doesn't seem to quite fit this explanation.

One night in Victorian times a wherry skipper called Tungate and his wife were walking home from Coldham Hall by moon- light. They glanced across to the meadow by the road and saw a bare-header waiter with a white tie and carrying a cloth napkin over his arm.

The waiter was keeping pace with them as they walked along the road. Strange - but the next bit had the hairs rising on the backs of their necks. The 'waiter' started gliding over ditches and hedges *without touching them...*

The fairy folk

Fortunately, not every folklore inhabitant of Norfolk is as nasty as Jack. There are a couple of tales about fairies - but even these Norfolk Tinkerbells had something strange about them.

Mrs Lubbock said: 'There used to be Fairies in old times. There are no such things now.'

But she told the story of a deep hole in the parish of Dilham called Seagar-ma-hole, which was thought to be a Fairies' bay. It had swallowed up a whole church - and several cattle unwise enough to stray into it.

Fairies would never appear in houses which were untidy - they hated dirt. A Victorian priest in Diss was told by his parish clerk that he knew 'several houses' where the fairies visited - but they never appeared when anyone was about.

Norfolk Giants

From the tiniest people in Norfolk folklore to the biggest...
and some real-life giants too...

The legend of Tom Hickathrift
The Marshland villages of Norfolk have this famous story,
which is certainly a very old legend. The King's Lynn historian
the Rev William Richards, writing in 1812, even thought it was
from before the Norman Conquest, although others say it
was Sir Henry Spelman who first wrote down the stories in
1630.

There are lots of
tales about Tom - here's
just a few.

Hickathrift (he was
sometimes called
'Hickifric') lived in
Tilney Fen End (where
there was a road called
Hickathrift's Drove).
One day Tom was
attacked by a gang of
robbers and he didn't
have a weapon of his own
- so tore off the wheel
of a cart to use as a
shield, and used the big
wooden axles that the
wheels were attached to
as a club! No prizes for
guessing who won that
particular contest.

Yes, he was a big chap, our Tom. In the garden of Hickathrift House at Marshland Smeeth there used to be a hollow about 25 metres wide - called 'Hickathrift's washbowl' - and another nearby hollow (which was a mere 14 metres across) was called 'Hickathrift's soap bowl'.

If Tom asked you for a favour it was a good idea to say 'yes' - in fact one version of the story has him as an evil fee-fi-fo-fum sort of giant - but it could ending up costing you dear, as a farmer discovered when Tom asked him if he could borrow a 'little straw' for his pig. He ended up carrying off the whole stack!

Tom, who if his supposed tomb (see over the page) is anything to go by was actually 'only' about 2.1m tall, once took on and beat a fearsome proper-sized giant at Wisbech - using the old 'cart wheel shield and club' trick.

Obviously word hadn't got round to the giant's neck of the woods.

Actually, talking about 'neck', that was what happened next - Tom knocked the giant's head clean off.

The evil giant is supposed to be buried in a mound called the Giant's Grave (but you'd guessed that, hadn't you?) which was near the old Smeeth Road rail station.

They could have done with Tom in the Marshland football team because, boy, could he boot the ball.

Two holes in the north and south walls of the chancel at Walpole St Peter parish church were blamed on Tom kicking a ball against it.

He surpassed even this one day when he said he would kick a stone ball and wherever it fell would be where he would be buried. He kicked it from Tilney St Lawrence to the wall of Tilney All Saints church - more than three kilometres away - and made a crack in the wall. Another version has Tom throwing his battleaxe all the way from King's Lynn.

Either way, under the crack is his grave...

The Norfolk Giant

Hickathrift might belong to the realms of folklore, but Norfolk can boast a real-life giant too.

The 'Norfolk Giant' - Robert Hales - was born at Somerton in 1820, part of a huge family. Huge in size, that is. Robert grew to be 7ft 6in (2.25m) tall and at 33 stones (nearly 210kg) was considered to be the biggest man in the Western world at the time.

People were much smaller then, so his father (at 6ft 6in) and mother (6ft) already attracted plenty of attention. In fact reports of Robert's death mentioned the claim that his mother was the descendant of a giant warder in Henry VIII's time who was supposed to have been 8ft 4in (2.54m) tall!

He started out as a sailor on the Broads, but they had to cut holes in the cabin to fit him in. He tried life in the Royal Navy - but he was too big for their ships too.

Eventually - inevitably - he ended up in the circus with his sister Mary (who was only a few centimetres shorter).

He sailed to the United States in 1848-9 to join the famous Barnum and Bailey Circus (diving overboard to save a child from drowning on the way).

He met Queen Victoria and Prince Albert and their children in 1851, who were fascinated by his story.

Robert later became the landlord of a London pub - we're guessing the customers were *very* well behaved - but his health got worse and he came back to Norfolk.

He died in November 1863, aged just 43. And you can visit his grave at St Mary's Church in West Somerton.

A prehistoric giant?
In 1665 the sea washed away part of the cliffs at Winterton, to reveal a monstrous bone 1.3m long and weighing 57lb (almost 26kg). Medical men who looked at the giant bone said it was a human thighbone... which would have made its owner, oh, around 10 feet (3.04m) tall!

...which sounds like a genuinely 'tall tale' to finish with.

Pathetic Play

Talking about Robert Hales' appearance in circuses is a link to this chapter, which takes a look at some equally unusual ways of being entertained. So read on as we...

...start Britain's first boy band

Yes, really. The very first secular (non-religious) English song with four-part harmony was the tune 'Summer is i-cumen in'. Its title basically means 'Hooray, summer's on the way!', which is a subject matter that's been popular with song-writers ever since.

And the local link? The tune was written down in the early 13th century at Reading Abbey by the monk John of Fornsete (Forncett in Norfolk).

And fans of slightly rude words will be delighted to know there's one in this song - in the line 'bullock starteth, buck farteth'.

OK, you can stop giggling now.

...imitate a pelican

The pelican is famous for having a huge beak in which it can stuff lots of food and liquid. So what better name for an old Swaffham drinking society? No-one could join the Pelican Club unless they could drink a quart (= 1.1 litres) of strong beer – in one go! Glug, glug, glug...

...be a cheat

There used to be a cruel old country 'sport' called cock-fighting (which we've mentioned in 'NASTY NORWICH' and 'NASTY NORFOLK') which basically involved setting male chickens to battle each other in a mini-arena.

Lots of people used to watch - and tons of money was bet on the outcome. So the temptation was there to cheat. Which was exactly what the naughty Norwich team did when they travelled to the Swan at Mattishall to take on the village chickens.

The Norwich team got at the Mattishall birds and 'smoked' them, by blowing lots of smoke over them - which left the chickens reeling about as if they were drunk.

We bet the feathers flew when the Mattishall chaps found out...

...stop anybody having any fun whatsoever

That was what seemed to be going on in Wells in the 1840s. The local councillors banned people from playing music in the streets, going for a swim in the sea after 10am (unless you'd changed in a tent), making slides on the ice or - and this must have been a *big* disappointment - beating a carpet before 9am.

...have a fireworks night turn tragic

And, yes, this is a genuinely nasty one. The street procession and fun known as the Norwich Pageant ended in disaster in 1611 when the fireworks caused a large series of explosions - which terrified a 'large number' of the spectators, making them trample others in their rush to escape.

...make a practical joke go wrong

Sir Astley Cooper was one of Norfolk's most respectable people in the 19th century. But when he was a boy growing up in Great Yarmouth, well, he was a little terror.

He was always playing practical jokes on people. Then one day, things didn't quite go the way he was expecting...

A Mr Francis Turner was talking to his apprentice when the boy suddenly burst out laughing and giggling uncontrollably. Turner looked behind his back - and saw young Cooper pulling stupid faces.

'What are you doing, boy?' he fumed at the lad.

Cooper clamped his hand to his mouth and made a few moaning noises going 'Oh my tooth, oh my tooth!' (Very smart, he thought to himself, just watch me get away with this).

Er, not really. Turner pulled Cooper's hand away from his mouth, reached in - and wrenched a tooth out.

Francis Turner, you see, was a surgeon - and a dentist.

A Gaggle of Ghosts

We've looked at lots of stories of spectres, ghouls and unexplained creepy things so far. For our last-but-one chapter let's dip back into the spooky drawer for one final mega-helping of horrible hauntings....

The Hickling Skater

One of the Broads' most famous spectral visitors is this chap. It's based on a story which is supposed to have happened during the Napoleonic Wars - when Britain was battling France and which ended with the 1815 Battle of Waterloo.

One night a soldier was skating over Hickling Broad to meet his lady love on the far side.

But he went over a thin patch - and the ice cracked, hurling him into the freezing water, where he drowned. His body was not found until the ice melted... weeks later.

And ever since, his ghost is supposed to glide over the broad....

The screams of Maude Gray

And another Napoleonic era tale, but this time from Norwich. This story is said to have taken place off St Benedict's and concerns a pregnant local woman who threw herself down a well when she heard her soldier love had been killed in the war.

Her ghostly cries are said to have been heard from down the well.

Possibly saying 'Hello up there, I've changed my mind, get me out of this !*&!!*&!! well!!'

The mystery of Magdalen Street

Number 19 (the former Red Lion pub) in the historic Norwich street was the site of a series of hauntings by a female ghost. People who worked at the building reported hearing footsteps and feeling mysterious draughts. Typewriters (which people used before computers) used to work by themselves too!

The ghost was supposed to be that of a woman - who had been murdered.

The return of Jimmy Cox

Here's another creepy story from the 19th century - and another from the Broads, which seems to be a great place for ghosts and spooky things...

There used to be a broadsman called Jimmy Cox, who lived at Barton.

He made his living by, among other things, running an eel-sett (fish trap) near Irstead Shoals.

Three weeks after his death, a wherryman called Waters stopped for the night at the shoals.

He was staggered to look up and see, sitting at the tiller of the barge, Jimmy Cox.

'Why, Jimmy, I thought you was dead,' he said (I think I would have gone 'AAAAAAARGH!!!!!'). Jimmy never said a word and just looked back at him - and Waters' nerve finally went. He grabbed a pole to quant (punt) the wherry away from the cursed spot.

He kept his eyes closed until he was well away from the shoals.

And he never went back - *ever*.

Another place the wherrymen tried to avoid - at least at night - was the old river bridge at Acle. There's a tradition that criminals were hanged over the middle arch for the birds and fish to nibble. Going under the arch on a spooky night was something for the brave - or the just plain stupid.

The Dereham hauntings
Sandy Lane in the town was a spooky place to be in the late 1960s and early 1970s - or at least that was what the rumours said.

The stories started around 1968 when a 15-year-old girl saw a man in 18th-century clothes in her bedroom... and she could see right through him. Terrified, she ran for safety into her mother's room.

Then a young woman was walking along the road in August 1969 when she saw a figure in front of her in Edwardian dress. She realised with shock that he was walking a foot above the ground.

The figure walked towards her and disappeared - bit by bit.

There was another claimed sighting in January 1972 - but the ghost was just down to a pair of legs this time!

Strange things at the Samson and Hercules
The Samson and Hercules is one of the best-known buildings in Norwich's Tombland.

It's been many things in its time - dancehall, nightclub and, earlier, as a centre for the YMCA (yes, as in 'it's fun to stay at...' etc).

In its YMCA days there was a certain room in which people who stayed had a recurring nightmare about being buried in a pit.

The story claimed that this part of the building had been built over a plague pit - where victims of the Black Death were thrown...

And next door the lovely old Augustine Steward House used to have a spooky resident - the Grey Lady. Stories of her ghostly visits were running until at least the 1970s.

She was another woman thought to be pining for her lover to come from the Napoleonic Wars.

The Ghost of the Rope Walk
A strange tale was told about this part of The Walks park at King's Lynn. In 1931 a man saw a figure huddled and lying on the path. As he moved closer the figure got up... and vanished into thin air. Spooky!

George's ghost
George Swain was a famous Norwich photographer who took many pictures recording the life of the city in the 20th century. But one thing he didn't manage to capture on film was a certain visitor to the Thorpe area.

George recalled in January 1964 how, when riding along on his motorbike, he used to see a black shape about the size of a dog come out of a grating 200 metres from the Red Lion pub, cross over the road - and disappear into the cemetery.

This always happened around 11.45pm. 'Always'? That's right - George reckoned he had seen the shape *18 times* in a 20-year period up to 1945.

He also reported having a prickly sensation at the back of his neck every time he saw it.

Well, you would, wouldn't you?

'I'm "grate" at haunting!'

The little old lady of Lyng...

...sounds like the first time to a poem, but is actually a story about a haunting in one of the village houses. Apparently the ghostly old woman was seen in a child's bedroom where she would always go to a certain wall. When the wall was investigated, a secret hole was discovered - with several gold sovereign coins inside (and you thought I was going to say 'skeleton', didn't you?).

The Beecheno Road haunting

And talking of ghostly old ladies, there was a mysterious case in Norwich in the early 1960s when a family was driven from its home after several years of bumps, ghostly apparitions - and screams. Experts from Cambridge University's Psychic Research Society even paid a visit to investigate - but could throw no light on the mystery.

But here's a strange thing: in December 1949 the ghost of a little old lady was also seen in Beecheno Road - but in a different house.

Silver-screen spooks

The former Regent cinema in Downham Market is supposed to have had at least two spooks - the 'Gainsborough Lady' (a posh 18th-century woman) and, more creepily, a man dressed in black on the stairs.

The airfield spooks

When you think of the thousands of pilots and air crew who have flown out of Norfolk in two world wars - and the many, many who didn't come back - it's understandable that there might be a spooky tale or two about them.

Here's a couple: the old control tower at Tibenham airfield (which was demolished in the early 1990s) was said to be haunted by the ghost of a US airman - and over in West Norfolk the Bircham Newton airfield (now the CITB) is said to have been visited by a phantom sports car, full of laughing airmen, who race across the base to crash into a hangar. There's also supposed to be the ghosts of three airmen in the squash courts - hauntings investigated over several years by the Anglia Society for Paranormal Research.

The Snettisham ghost

One of the strangest spooky stories of Norfolk - and certainly one of the best-investigated - happened in 1893.

A London woman, a Mrs Goodeve, was visiting friends in Bristol when she woke one night to see a sad but kindly old woman who told her to follow her into the next room where she said 'Tomorrow' - and vanished.

The next morning she asked if anyone knew of the ghost and was told it matched the description of a former occupant, Mrs Seagrim. Mrs S did return later that night, told her what date she had married, and was suddenly joined by another spook who said his name was Henry Barnard.

Barnard told Mrs Goodeve that he was buried in Snettisham churchyard and that she had to go there to take a white rose from the grave of a man called Robert Cobbs.

Mrs Goodeve carried out her mission - travelling to Snettisham (which she had never heard of before), finding the graves - and picking the rose.

The Snettisham parish clerk, John Bishop, agreed to let her into the church at 1am.

She was joined by his wife Agnes while Mr Bishop himself waited outside.

The two women never said what happened inside - but the clerk later told his grandchild that he had heard a man's voice coming from the vestry...

The case was investigated by the Society for Psychical Research, who described Mrs Goodeve as 'a cheerful, capable, active women...by no means given to dwelling on things morbid or mysterious.'

Haunted Hoaxes

For our final chapter we take a look at some spooky stories which were not quite what they seemed... or were they?

The Heigham Street Ghost

In the 1880s this spook terrorised the women who lived in this Norwich road. They would walk down the streets with their shawls over their heads and carrying their shopping baskets - but when they passed the former workhouse an old woman, dressed in another shawl, would leap on their backs and steal their money.

But the 'haunting' came to a sudden end when two of the would-be victims turned out to be men who had dressed up as their womenfolk to catch the 'ghost'.

After giving the very human thief (because, of course, that's who it was) a good thumping, they handed him over to the police.

"I haven't the ghost of a chance!'

Sticks and stones...

Around 1929 a figure in white was seen in King's Avenue in King's Lynn - with the residents of one house hit by mud and stones. But the local police soon worked out that the 'ghost' was a naughty boy rather than a naughty spook...

The Syderstone haunting
In 1833 the Norfolk public was fascinated by reports of
mysterious hauntings in the village parsonage.

The Rev Stewart heard strange knockings in the night,
running from 2am to daylight. Every night the knocking grew
louder, until one of the servants could stand it no longer and
fled in terror.

The sounds came from the ceiling, walls and floor,
sometimes with the sound of moaning and the rattling of
chains. The house was carefully searched but nothing was
found.

Several people went to check on the reports. Here's what
they found: 'Especial care was taken that no tricks should be
played by the servants; but the noises were even louder and
longer than usual.

'They commenced in Miss Stewart's bedchamber, and
three powerful knocks were given to the sideboard whilst the
hand of Mr Goggs was upon it.'

These noises 'continued from between 11 and 12 o'clock,
until nearly two hours after sunrise...'

But eventually it was discovered that the 'haunting' was a
carefully-arranged hoax after all.

The Swanton Novers poltergeist
But an alleged haunting of another Norfolk rectory almost a
century later became a much more celebrated incident.

The EDP in August 1919 reported the story under the
headline 'A Norfolk Oil Mystery', beginning its report with
the words 'A singular and mysterious state of things prevails
at the rectory of Swanton Novers...'

This is what was happening: in early August the Rev Hugh
Guy and his family had noticed a faint smell of petrol or
paraffin after slight earth tremors.

But unconcerned, they had gone off on holiday.

When they returned they found furniture drenched in the stinky liquids. Baffled, they took up the floorboards and plaster - and found they were dry.

In early September, a church architect visited the rectory to see for himself and said: 'There does not seem to be any reasonable explanation. In fact there is something uncanny about it.'

'This is a problem not to be sniffed at!'

By this time the story was attracting national attention, and was described as 'one of the most famous puzzles of its kind that has ever afflicted a county rectory'.

With the oil dripping almost daily by now, there came an unexpected investigator on the scene - a magician.

Oswald Williams and his wife Rae happened to be staying at Cromer when they heard about the mystery.

Smelling a case of trickery, the magician called at the house to investigate.

First, he cut off all possible supplies of water to the house - then noticed that oil splashes seemed to happen when the young maidservant went out of the room and came back 'looking very pleased with herself'.

Then the magician caught the girl splashing water up at the ceiling - and the servant confessed she had been behind the 'haunting'.

But a day later the mystery returned, when the 14-year-old girl, who was called Mabel Phillipo, claimed that, no, she had never really confessed at all.

The girl was sent home anyway - and the incidents stopped. But some people have claimed that young Mabel had somehow brought to life a poltergeist - a kind of spirit...

The Christmas Eve ghost
Our final tale is one where a prank backfired - with tragic results.

During the 1860s, the writer Ernest Suffling was in a (unnamed) Norfolk village to mend a stained glass window. He left for the comfort of the local pub on Christmas Eve, leaving behind two workmen, Joe Canham and George Cole, and the church sexton, Solomon Hannet.

Suffling was woken up in the early hours of Christmas morning by the landlord of the pub, who took him downstairs to meet Solomon, who was overcome with terror.

He told Suffling that George had vanished.

The two men went back to the church where they found George - dead, apparently from a terrible shock.

The sexton explained that they had been terrified after an apparition, with white fangs and carrying a human skull, came after them in the church.

If you're wondering what hap-pened to Joe in all this, you weren't alone.

But it wasn't until nearly a year later that the true story came out.

'Say what you like, there's something spooky going on here!'

Joe was on his own deathbed when he finally admitted to Suffling what had happened.

It had been him pretending to be a ghost... and scarily enough to kill his workmate stone dead.

Well that's the final story to tell. We hope you've enjoyed your visit to the spooky side of Nasty Norfolk (and the juicy bits of nasty history we've included too). Don't forget that these are all just stories, though, so there's no need to be frightened and... hang on, I'll just answer that knock at the door...

...wait a minute, there's no-one there!
MUMMY! FIND ME MY TEDDY!!!!!

Meet the author

TREVOR HEATON is the author, co-author or editor of several books on Norfolk, including Images of Norfolk, Norfolk Century and Images of King's Lynn. He was also the co-author of a cartoon strip in The Journalist magazine, and his work also features in The Oldie Book of Cartoons.

He studied archaeology at school and university, and is a journalist for the Eastern Daily Press.

He was the winner of a 2006 British Archaeological Award for his "Treasure Your Past" magazine, produced in association with the British Museum and Norwich Castle.

Nasty Norfolk: Scary Tales and Ghastly Ghosts is the third in his "Nasty..." series of local best-sellers.

If you've enjoyed this book, then why not tell your friends – and check out Nasty Norwich and Nasty Norfolk.

And if you haven't........ SHHHHHHH!